COLUMBIA UNIVERSITY LECTURES

SOCIAL EVOLUTION AND POLITICAL THEORY

BY

LEONARD T. HOBHOUSE

PROFESSOR OF SOCIOLOGY IN THE UNIVERSITY OF LONDON

New York
COLUMBIA UNIVERSITY PRESS
1922

All rights reserved

COPYRIGHT, 1911,
BY COLUMBIA UNIVERSITY PRESS.

Set up and electrotyped. Published November, 1911. Reprinted November, 1913; January, 1922.

Norwood Press
J. S. Cushing Co. — Berwick & Smith Co.
Norwood, Mass., U.S.A.

NOTE

THE present volume contains the substance of eight lectures given on the Beer Foundation under the Faculty of Political Science of Columbia University during April, 1911. The lecture form is preserved, but with additions which necessitate a division into nine chapters. A portion of the argument of Chapter VI is set out in more detail in the writer's "Morals in Evolution," and the subject of Chapter IX is treated under a somewhat different aspect in a recent volume on "Liberalism" in the "Home and University Library."

TO THE FACULTY OF POLITICAL SCIENCE:

May I take this opportunity of expressing my gratitude to the members of the Faculty of Political Science of Columbia University, and to the Trustees of the Beer Foundation for an experience of deep and abiding interest? I cannot flatter myself that I could teach your students very much in the brief course of lectures here reprinted, but I am certain that I, on my side, learned a great deal. The freshness, the vitality, the largeness of conception, the intellectual as well as social hospitality that characterize American academic life, have been to me stimulating and invigorating beyond all expectation. I can wish nothing better to those who follow me on the Beer Foundation than that they should receive an impression as fortunate and profound.

Very sincerely yours,
L. T. HOBHOUSE.

GRINDELWALD, July 26, 1911.

CONTENTS

CHAPTER		PAGE
I.	THE MEANING OF PROGRESS	1
II.	PROGRESS AND THE STRUGGLE FOR EXISTENCE	17
III.	THE VALUE AND LIMITATIONS OF EUGENICS	40
IV.	SOCIAL HARMONY AND THE SOCIAL MIND	80
V.	SOCIAL MORPHOLOGY	102
VI.	THE GROWTH OF THE STATE	126
VII.	EVOLUTION AND PROGRESS	149
VIII.	SOCIAL PHILOSOPHY AND MODERN PROBLEMS	166
IX.	THE INDIVIDUAL AND THE STATE	185

SOCIAL EVOLUTION AND POLITICAL THEORY

CHAPTER I

THE MEANING OF PROGRESS

LIKE every age and every state of human society the period in which we live has its merits and defects, its elements of success and failure. Contemporary critics assuming the part of candid friends are perhaps more concerned with the failures, and the note of pessimism sounds clearly enough in much of the literature of the day. But depreciation of the present, gloomy views of the future, and idealization of the past are common characteristics of literary criticism. If literature is evidence, we could construct a chain of testimony proving the continuous deterioration of humanity from the time of Hesiod to the present day. The past, when it is seen at all, appears always in a halo of romance. Just as in our own personal memory many things which we should be exceedingly loath to experience anew become positively enjoyable in the mellowness of retrospect, as the contrast of some great hardship forms a pleasing background for present comfort, so in the memory of the race much that we should be sorry to live through again in real earnest acquires the tinge of romance when viewed at a safe distance. Whereas the discomforts, the ugliness, and the squalor of the present afflict us with all the insistence of grim reality, the corresponding elements in the past are either forgotten or are softened and transfigured by the haze of time. Hence it is that our view of historical change tends to be distorted in the direction of pessimism, and in any attempt at a scientific measure of social progress we must be on our guard against this bias of social memory. Those who are most zealous for social improvement will indeed be the last to minimize the evils that exist. But without yielding to any such temptation there is, I would suggest, one compensatory element of which the prevalence of a somewhat pessimistic criticism is itself the proof. There was probably never a time at which among civilized peoples there was so much diffused sensitiveness to any form of social ailment. If we were briefed to defend our own time, the line to take would surely be, not that its evils are few or small, but rather that every evil calls forth a strong and persistent effort to cure it. Such effort is not indeed new, but it may be fairly maintained that it persists and grows in volume and seriousness, that it enlists an increasing proportion of human effort and ability, and that as it gathers strength and substance it is less content to deal with symptoms and effects, and becomes more intent on the discovery and eradication of causes. In every civilized country there is an army of men and women at work, some trusting to voluntary effort and mutual aid, others pinning their faith to governments and agitating for legislative reforms, and yet others content for the time to investigate facts, examine into causes, and pave the way for a more assured progress in the future. The pessimistic writer will not deny the existence or the sincerity of these manifold forms of social effort, but it is open to him to question their efficiency. On this point a good deal might be said. I think it would be possible, so far at least as my own country is concerned, to show by a series of comparisons of the condition of the people in the earlier stages of the industrial revolution with their condition at the present day that the efforts of the reformers have not been wasted. I shall not, however, attempt this task at present, for I am going instead to make an admission. If my supposed critic were to scrutinize the terms in which I described the efforts of reformers, there is one word on which he might fasten with some effect. I spoke of "an army of men and women." "What army?" he might reply. "I see clearly enough, great numbers of men and women who interest themselves in public questions. But an army means a drilled and organized force, moving towards a clear objective. This," he might say, "is precisely what I do not find among the enthusiasts for social reform. What I find is something much more like a mob, or, if we are to keep to military metaphors, something like a miscellaneous assortment of guerilla bands, acting without concert, often at cross purposes, sometimes coming into violent conflict, and at best with no clear sense of any common cause. There are individuals and organized bodies, if you will, who concentrate their energies on temperance, but who concentrate so completely that they care for nothing else. There are those who combat pauperism and preach thrift. There are enthusiasts who find land questions at the root of all good and all evil. There are the apostles of housing and sanitary reform. There are Tariff Reformers — an expression which has, so to say, opposite signs in England and the United States. There are Trade Unionists, Cooperators, Socialists, and again there is the insistent school of Eugenists, who treat all social reforms as mere subsidiary changes of the environment and insist that the modification of the race by selection is the only matter of vital moment. In a word there are thousands and tens of thousands vaguely interested in social progress, and keenly interested in some particular question which has come within the field of their special experience or to which they have been led to give personal attention. Here and there is to be found a broader-minded person who recognizes the wholeness of things, but his influence is small. The driving force is all with the sectional spirit, and that is why you get little or no general progress."

With one part of this indictment I should agree. Notwithstanding all narrowness and short-sightedness I think that something has been done, but it has been done at the expense of a vast and disproportionate waste of effort. If this waste is to be avoided and the aggregate of social effort is now to have the measure of success which it deserves, it must be through the growth of a common understanding, through the emergence of clearer ideas of social progress as a whole, and by consequence of the mutual relations of its constituent parts. People are apt to turn from such questions as abstract and academic, but there are seemingly academic questions which are charged with very real meaning, and the unity of social organisms and the interrelation for good and for evil of social changes is no mere form of words, but a way of expressing a deep-seated truth which those who ignore it will in practice strike on sooner or later. You may remember a certain simile employed by Mr. Herbert Spencer in his "Study on Sociology." Give a man a sheet of metal with a dint in it, he says, and ask him to flatten it out. What does he do? If he knows nothing of metal work, he takes a hammer and knocks the dint flat, only to find that it has reappeared elsewhere. He applies the hammer again at the new point with the same result, and so he goes on till he convinces himself that dints are not to be levelled out by this direct and easy method. So it is, urges Mr. Spencer, with society. We find some evil or evils which we seek to prevent by direct and forcible means, only to find, says this critic of social effort, that a corresponding evil appears somewhere else. We put down overt crime only to find that some form of secret vice is increasing. A temperance crusade suppresses drunkenness, and it is discovered that those who used to drink now find an outlet for excitement in gambling. Compensation for accidents is secured by law to workmen, and in consequence it is alleged that elderly workmen are refused situations. Workmen form trade unions to maintain and improve the conditions of their work, and no sooner do they succeed than their employers imitate them and form federations by which the unions are overpowered. Strikes are replaced by mutual agreements which are to initiate an era of industrial peace, and it is found that the wider the agreement the less it meets the local difficulties of mine and workshop, and we see workmen striking substantially against their own leaders. I need not here inquire whether in all these instances the allegation is correct, nor whether even if that be so there may not be some net gain. I am concerned only with the simple and preliminary point, to which Mr. Spencer did well to call attention, that every change, however good in itself, provokes unforeseen reactions, and that if we are to achieve permanent and assured good we must as far as possible keep in view the life of society as a whole and seek not jealously to magnify our own little sectional interest at the expense of the others, but rather to correlate it with the work that others are doing and endeavor to induce in them the same spirit. In sociology as in all sciences specialism is a necessity and it is also a danger. It is a necessity for the simple reason that human capacity is limited and it is not given to man to acquire sound knowledge and adequate skill in many departments at once. It is a danger because social life is no more divisible into independent sections than the human body is divisible into independent organisms. Now the belief that "there is nothing like leather" is *mutato nomine* universal. To exaggerate the importance of what one is doing oneself is the necessary human illusion. It is the stimulant which sustains. Unfortunately it is also the stimulant which intoxicates, and in sober mood we may well engage ourselves in the effort to find some prophylactic. In the present case the prophylactic that we need, if I am right, is an articulate social philosophy. We ought to inquire whether underlying the diffused mass of social effort there is discoverable any coherent scheme of social betterment or progress as a whole. If again we can find any such general conception, we have to ask whether it will hold water, and this will divide

itself into two main questions. Before we can decide
whether any purpose which men may propound to themselves is valid and reasonable we must determine, first, whether it is self-consistent, or whether if thought out it would evolve any contradictions which would reduce it to meaningless confusion; and secondly, whether it lies within the limits of practical possibility. The first of these questions is the subject-matter of social philosophy, the second belongs to the theory of social evolution. I shall not be able within the compass of these lectures to deal with either question with the fullness which it deserves, but for reasons which will appear as we proceed I cannot limit myself to one alone. I shall therefore (1) attempt a summary definition of the nature and conditions of progress, and shall proceed (2) to consider how far progress as defined has actually been realized in history, and how far it is capable of further and future realization. In place of an attempt to cover the whole ground in a summary which would necessarily be vague and thin, I shall, both in dealing with past and present, confine myself in the main to one side of social life, merely glancing at others when the progress of the argument makes it necessary to do so.

There are, however, certain difficulties which the conception of progress meets at the outset, and it will be better to deal with these before proceeding to our constructive argument.

For this purpose I will ask you to be content with a rough preliminary definition of progress, and let me do what I can within my limits to make it a little more precise at a later stage. Now you will have noticed that I have used the term "evolution" in regard to human society and also the term "progress." This should imply that there is some difference between them, and in point of fact, to grasp this difference is in my view the beginning of understanding in these matters. By evolution I mean any sort of growth; by social progress, the growth of social life in respect of those qualities to which human beings attach or can rationally attach value. Social progress, then, is only one among many possibilities of social evolution. At least it is not to be assumed that any and every form of social evolution is also a form or a stage in social progress. For example, a caste system is a product of social evolution, and the more rigid and narrow the caste, the more complex the hierarchy, the more completely has the caste system evolved. In proportion, that is, as a loose and incipient caste system hardens into an extreme and rigid caste system, there is a distinct process of social evolution going forward; but most of us would question very strongly whether it could be considered in any sense as a phase of social progress. Judged from the standpoint of human values, it looks more like retrogression, or perhaps still more like divergence into a side track, from which there is no exit save by going back over a good deal of the ground travelled. So again there is at the present day a vigorous evolution of cartels, monopolies, rings, and trusts; there is an evolution of imperialism, of socialism, of nationalism, of militarism, in a word, of a hundred tendencies as to the good or evil of which people differ. The fact that a thing is evolving is no proof that it is good, the fact that society has evolved is no proof that it has progressed. The point is important because under the influence of biological conceptions the two ideas are often confused, and the fact that human beings have evolved under certain conditions is treated as evidence of the value of those conditions, or perhaps as proving the futility of ethical ideas which run counter to evolutionary processes. Thus in an article by a clever exponent of eugenic principles I find a contemptuous reference to "the childlike desire to make things 'fair,' which is so clearly contrary to the order of a universe which progresses by natural selection."[1] In this brief remark you will observe two immense assumptions, and one stark contradiction. The first assumption is that the universe progresses — not humanity, observe, nor the mass of organic beings, nor even the earth, but the universe. The second assumption is that it progresses by natural selection, a hypothesis which has not yet adequately explained the bare fact of the variation of organic forms on the surface of this earth. The contradiction is that progress is incompatible with fairness, the basic element in all judgments of value, so that we are called upon to recognize as valuable that by which our fundamental notions of value are set at naught. It may be replied that the process of things has nothing to do with human ideas of value. That of course is perfectly possible, and is the point we shall have to examine. But in that case no one has a right to speak of progress, a term which connotes value, in relation to the process of things. If there exist laws of mechanical necessity which involve the defeat of human effort based on human judgments of value, then it is true that human effort must be forever frustrate, but it is untrue that human effort must seek to ally itself with its en-

[1] Mr. W. C. D. Whetham in the *Eugenic Review*, Nov. 1910.

emy. If the process of the universe is inherently opposed to the ethical order, it follows that the ethical order is inherently opposed to the process of the universe. In this state of things the position of humanity would be very unfortunate. It could not hope to achieve any permanent good. But it would still be the height of unreason for humanity to throw its efforts for whatever they may be worth on the side of those forces which by hypothesis are working against the best elements in its life. The only rational course in so bad a situation would be first to see what could be saved from the wreck, or, if nothing could be done, then to remain passive and endure with what patience we could command. Why we should take active pains to forward a process which conflicts with our fundamental conceptions of what is valuable is a question which answers itself.

Of course this is not the way in which the question ordinarily presents itself. By studying certain sides of organic evolution people arrive at a particular hypothesis of the nature of the process. They erect this hypothesis into an universal and necessary law, and straightway call upon every one else to acknowledge the law and conform to it in action. Unaccustomed to philosophical analysis, and contemptuous of that to which they are unaccustomed, they do not see that they have passed from one sense of law to another, that they have confused a generalization with a command, and a statement of facts with a principle of action. They accordingly miss the starting-point from which a distinct conception of progress and its relation to human effort becomes possible. But for any useful theory of the bearing of evolution on social effort this conception is vital. We can get no light upon the subject unless we begin with the clear perception that the object of social effort is the realization of ends to which human beings can reasonably attach value, that is to say, the realization of ethical ends; and this being understood, we may suitably use the term "progress" of any steps leading towards such realization. Now it may be said that human valuations are themselves often obscure, confused, and contradictory. That is, in fact, the reason why we need a social philosophy to reduce them to a rational order. But we are not asking for the moment what the rational judgment of man would approve. We are contending for the preliminary point, that without its approval there can be no talk of progress, that to hold up a process to admiration, to praise it as good, to accept and forward it, is, in fact, to pass on it a judgment of approval, and that to do these things and in the same breath to scorn the principle which is the pivot of any ethical approval is a contradiction. If this and allied principles are false and meaningless, that requires independent proof. If justice, fairness, mutual aid, benevolence, pity, are inherently confused and contradictory ideas, they cannot serve as bases of rational approval or disapproval. But this has to be demonstrated, and there is no beginning of demonstration in the mere fact that such qualities as these are opposed to the naked struggle for existence.

Our conclusion so far is that the nature of social progress cannot be determined by barely examining the actual conditions of social evolution. Evolution and progress are not the same thing. They may be opposed. They might even be so fundamentally opposed that progress would be impossible, and whether this is so is one of the two questions which we distinguished above, and which I shall proceed to discuss. I take occasion only to remind you that the other question was — In what does progress consist? and to this we have given the preliminary answer that it means the realization of an ethical order; and we have now further seen that the nature of this order is not to be determined by asking whether it conforms to natural processes, but by asking whether it yields rational and coherent guidance to human effort. To this question we shall come in due course. We have now to deal with the preliminary question whether in the light of the facts of life the idea of progress as an advancing realization of an ethical order can be regarded as a valid idea. That is to say, is progress possible? If so, social effort has an intelligible and self consistent goal. If not, it is doomed to self-defeat.

The optimistic view encounters many objections. One is founded on history, or more widely on a comparative survey of human society, which suggests the doubt whether for the mass of mankind any substantial progress has as yet been realized. Comparing the life of the savage with that of the civilized man, it maintains that the advantages are by no means all on one side, and, to put the view moderately, it urges that if all the centuries of effort that part the civilized man from his rude ancestors have produced such dubious results, we can hope very little from continuance on the same path. Unless we have some new fact to produce which is to initiate some wonder-working change, the lower we fix our expectations the less disappointed we shall be. A variant of this view founds itself more particularly on the history of civilization. It calls attention to the ups and downs of humanity. It points to the flower of Greek, of Roman, of medieval civilization, and to their subsequent decay. It questions whether we have advanced beyond them, or have built on firmer foundations, and it bids us prepare for a similar dissolution. These are questions of social evolution which require very careful examination. I shall endeavor in a later lecture to indicate the lines upon which I think they may be profitably discussed. But there is another and more fundamental objection to which I will first call your attention. This is derived from the biological conditions of human society.

The biological argument has taken more than one shape and may best be treated here by a brief historical retrospect. Its appearance in the arena of controversy was announced by the terrible douche of cold water thrown by Malthus on the speculative optimism of the eighteenth century. The generation preceding the French Revolution was a time of buoyant and sanguine outlook. There floated before men the idea of an Age of Reason that was near at hand, when mankind should throw off the incubus of the past and resume a life in accordance with nature in a social order founded on a rational consideration of natural rights. Nature both in the politics and the economics of the time assumes a half personal and wholly benevolent character, while human restrictions, human conventions, play the part of the villain in the piece. At this point Malthus intervened by calling attention to a "natural" law of great significance. This was the law that human beings multiplied in a geometrical ratio; that it was only by the checks of famine, pestilence, and war that they were prevented from overspreading the earth, and that, to cut the matter short, whatever the available means of subsistence mankind would always, in the absence of prudential checks, multiply up to the limit at which those means became inadequate. True, the means of subsistence might be extended. New countries might be opened up. New industrial processes might be invented, new sources of food supply discovered. Every such extension of the means of living, the Malthusian argued, would only redouble the rate of multiplication. The checks would cease, infants would cease to die. Men and women would marry earlier, and soon after each extension of the food supply we should find the population pressing as hard as ever upon the barriers. The advance of civilization told in the same direction. The suppression of violent deaths, the progress of sanitation — fortunately for their peace of mind the early Malthusians lived before the sanitary era — the decline of war, the improvement of public order, all tended to survival. Population was increasing, must increase, and could not be diminished. It could only be held in check by the one great barrier of the subsistence limit against which the fringe of advancing population must forever beat in misery. There could be no solution of the social question. For in the nature of things there must be a line where the surf of the advancing tide breaks upon the shore, and that shore was death from insufficiency of nourishment. You observe that in summarizing the argument I speak partly of Malthus, partly of the Malthusians. Malthus himself, particularly in his second edition, laid stress on the prudential checks, and he cannot fairly be accused of fostering the pessimistic views often fastened upon him. But for many a long year after he wrote, the efficacy of the prudential checks appeared to be very slight. It was his first edition that was generally absorbed and that profoundly affected social thought for nearly a century. Down to my own time the Malthusian theory, as interpreted above, appeared to be the principal crux of social progress. It was not till the seventies that there came into operation that general fall in the birth-rate, which has justified Malthus against the Malthusians, has put the calculations of the future growth of population on a radically different basis, and has brought about among other things a complete reconstruction of the biological argument against progress. With this argument I shall deal in due order, but I venture to think in the meantime that we may learn a lesson from the fate of Malthusianism. Mathematical arguments drawn from the assumption that human actions proceed with the statistical regularity that might be found in a flock of sheep are often exceedingly difficult to refute in detail, and yet they rest on an insecure foundation. Man is not merely an animal. He is also a rational being, and accordingly he reacts to new circumstances in a way that can only be determined by taking the possibility of rational purpose into account. The Malthusian theory was one cause of the defeat of its own prophecies. It was the belief that the population was growing too fast that operated indirectly to check its growth. Those who fear that the population is now growing too slowly may take some comfort from the reflection. We are not hastily to assume inevitable tendencies in human societies, because the moment that society is aware of its tendencies a new fact is introduced. Man, unlike other animals, is moved by the knowledge of ends, and can and does correct the tendencies whose results he sees to be disastrous. The alarmist talk of race suicide may serve its purpose if only by admonishing us of the fate of a social theory based on what appeared to be a most convincing biological calculation.

But long before the decline of the birth-rate set in, the biological argument had taken a completely new form. The conception of evolution had arisen, and had begun to exert a profound influence on thought in general and on social theory in particular. The conception of progress encountered new difficulties, and to them we must now turn.

CHAPTER II

Progress and the Struggle for Existence

The conception of evolution is inseparably, and not unjustly, associated in our minds with the work of Darwin and the impulse given by him in the middle of the nineteenth century to biological investigation. Yet, as we all know, the conception of evolution is not confined to biology, nor in biology did it originate with Darwin. Systematic attempts to treat social evolution in particular, and to treat it moreover by distinctly sociological methods, were familiar to the generation preceding the publication of the "Origin of Species." Under the title of the "Philosophy of History" attempts were made in Germany, in France, and in England to arrive at an interpretation of the record which should exhibit the succession of social phenomena as the working out in human society of permanent laws or tendencies. Premature as these efforts may have been, they have at least the merit of seeking the explanation of social phenomena in the nature of society itself. Comte and Buckle in particular, whatever may be said in criticism of the use which they made of their data, were at any rate convinced that those data lay within the records of humanity and were not to be provided for the sociologist by some more general science. In this respect the work of Darwin may be said to have cut across the normal and natural development of sociological investigation. When a great impulse is given to one science by some epoch-making experiment or some new and fruitful generalization, that science is apt to acquire a certain prestige in the minds of contemporaries, which gives it an influence over thought in every department, particularly in those departments where inquiry is still a novelty and where there is no fixed tradition to regulate the methods of approach.

Though Darwin was by no means the founder of the theory of biological evolution, he does occupy in the genesis of this theory a position not incomparable to that of Newton in the theory of the solar system. For if he did not invent the evolutionary hypothesis nor yet prove that hypothesis to be a demonstrable truth, he first, by amassing a vast store of material and by illuminating it with clear and simple conceptions drawn directly from experience, brought the hypothesis into contact with the facts and consolidated it as a basis for future investigation. He brought down evolution, as it were, from the clouds of speculation and established between it and the data of observation that kind of contact which alone can make an hypothesis a serious working force in the growth of science.

This is not the place for a discussion of the Darwinian theory, but one point which has an important bearing on the subsequent development of sociological method must be noted. Cautiously as Darwin expressed the principle of Natural Selection and fully as he recognized the possibility that other factors might have influence upon organic development, the main effect of his work in the world of science was to generate the conception of the progress of organic forms by means of a continuous struggle for existence wherein those best fitted by natural endowment to cope with their surroundings would tend, upon the whole, to survive. The persistence of this process and the consequent accumulation of the small variations that occur in every generation were the considerations on which he principally relied in explaining the vast differences which separate species from species, genus from genus, order from order, and class from class. Now if such a process could, in the course of ages, span the gulf that separates the rhizopod from the man, what need was there, it might be urged, of further factors in human progress. Man after all, in spite of his philosophy, was still an animal, still subject to the same laws of reproduction and variation, still modifiable in the same manner by the indirect selection of the individuals best fitted to their environment. Here, it was held, was a cause at work underlying all the relatively superficial factors which loom so large in history; here was a principle which would at last make sociology a science by connecting it with the established and acknowledged sciences of the physical world; here was an eminently modern conception which would take the treatment of social facts out of the hands of the literary historian or the rhetorical publicist, and establish the investigation of social progress upon the firm foundation of physical science. The true method of approaching the social questions for the future was to be — not the study of history, not the analysis of the fundamental social conceptions, not the examination of social institutions, not the comparative sciences of law, or religion, or ethics—but rather the investigation by biological methods of the nature and variation of human faculty, the exact ascertainment of the laws of heredity, and the statistical determination of the way in which variations propagated by heredity would affect the social stock. If it could be shown that height and chest-capacity and length of limb were hereditary qualities, so also it might be shown that cranial capacity, and with it mental and moral equipment, were equally handed on from parent to child. The true problem of social betterment was to determine the conditions under which the better qualities are propagated and the worse repressed. As to the general nature of these conditions, indeed, there could be no doubt for the biologist. He came to the science of society with this fundamental question already settled. He had not, like the philosopher, to trouble himself about what was best; nor, like the social investigator, to remain in doubt as to the broadest principles regulating the life of society. On both these questions his doubts were already solved by what he had learned in biology itself. The best was that which survived, and the persistent elimination of the least fit was the one method generally necessary to assure the survival of the best. Armed with this generalization the biologist found himself able to view the world at large — what Mr. Whetham calls, as we saw, the process of the universe — with much complacency. Life was constantly and necessarily growing better. In every species the least fit were always being destroyed and the standard of the survivors proportionately raised. No doubt there remained even in human society many features which are at first sight objectionable. But here again the evolutionist was in the happy position of being able to verify the existence of a soul of goodness in things evil. Was there acute industrial competition? It was the process by which the fittest came to the top. Were the losers in the struggle left to welter in dire poverty? They would the sooner die out. Were housing conditions a disgrace to civilization? They were the natural environment of an unfit class, and the means whereby such a class prepared the way for its own extinction. Was infant mortality excessive? It weeded out the sickly and the weaklings. Was there pestilence or famine? So many more of the unfit would perish. Did tuberculosis claim a heavy toll? The tubercular germs are great selectors, skilled at probing the weak spots of living tissue. Were there wars and rumors of wars? War alone would give to the conquering race its due, the inheritance of the earth. It would maintain the efficiency of the stronger and erase the less fit from the roll of nations. In a word the only blot that the evolutionist could see upon the picture was the misguided enthusiasm, the "maudlin sentiment," to use a favorite expression, which seeks to hold out a hand to those who are down, and to prolong the life of those who are proved unfit to exist by the fact of their ill success in the struggle. The one sinner against progress is the man who tries to save the lamb from the wolf. Could we abolish this unscientific individual, the prospects of the world would be unclouded.

I am putting this theory in language of my own, and it may seem a little harsh. The most scientifically minded among us retain traces of the "maudlin sentiment" in which we are bred, and which makes us hesitate to draw out our arguments to their logical conclusion. It is the more necessary that the legitimate inferences to be drawn from these hints and half-statements should be quite nakedly set forth, so that we may see precisely whither we are being led. And I think that the view which I have stated is clearly implied, if only half expressed, in much of the biological criticism of society from the time of Mr. Herbert Spencer to the present day. Not only so, but it is the logically inevitable consequence of the principles on which that criticism is founded. If by the "fit" we mean those who are best adapted by their own personal qualities to survive unaided in the struggle for life — and this is the sense in which the term is actually taken — then the consequences which have been indicated follow as does night the day. But they carry with them a very curious result. Every sort of aid given by one person to another will clearly tend, so far as it goes, to neutralize the inherent weakness of the person who is helped. Those who might perish if left to themselves may clearly through the aid of others be preserved through youth to maturity, and so be enabled in their turn to bring children into the world. Thus it would seem that through mutual aid the weaker stocks, which without it would be extinguished, may be enabled to propagate themselves, and the action of natural selection, which, eliminating the weaker stock, keeps the race strong, is in so far defeated. But if natural selection is the foundation of all progress, it follows that mutual aid is the persistent enemy of progress; and we arrive at the result that the more highly organized the common life of society the more surely is it destined to decay. Not only so — we must not suppose the process to set in only when society has reached a high stage of organization, for every successive step, which tends to substitute peace for war, agreement for conflict, forbearance for internecine struggle, has point by point involved a further restriction in the operation of natural selection, a weakening of the one force that makes for progress. Indeed, this process begins before human society is reached. Far down in the animal world we see — to go no farther — the operation of parental love keeping alive the callow young which could not exist for a day without maternal care. And stage by stage, as we ascend the animal kingdom and reach the level of humanity, we find this care developed so that from the first days of immaturity it extends throughout months and years of childhood. Yet, stage by stage as these and other forms of mutual aid extend, the resulting form of life is that which we ordinarily call "higher." Before we apply biological conceptions to social affairs, we generally suppose that the highest ethics is that which expresses the completest mutual sympathy and the most highly evolved society, that in which the efforts of its members are most completely coördinated to common ends, in which discord is most fully subdued to harmony. Accordingly we are driven to one of two alternatives. Either our valuations are completely false, our notions of higher and lower unmeaning, or progress, the process of betterment, does not depend on the naked struggle for existence. The biologist would cheerfully accept the first alternative. As we have already seen, he is disposed to tell us that we vainly seek to distort truth by importing our ethical standards. He is quite ready to insist that we must subordinate our judgments of value to the survival test. We must judge good that which succeeds. Unfortunately for him, at that stage his whole theory becomes a barren tautology. Progress now in his view results from the survival of the fittest, because progress is the process wherein the fittest survive. Again it is always the fittest who survive, because the fact of their survival proves their fitness. This purely verbal argument underlies a good deal of biological reasoning and often comes very near to the surface.

But in point of fact we have very sufficient reason to decline the biological alternative. The conceptions of human happiness, of mental development, of social co-operation, which lie at the root of the idea of progress are not meaningless. They require, no doubt, any amount of examination and criticism, and to work out all their implications is the standing task of social philosophy. Just as much may be said of any of the current terms of our common knowledge. But the first step in such an examination is to put the problem in its right shape, and the present problem is hopelessly misstated when a term like "fit," which suggests adaptation to some desirable end, is employed without so much as an effort to determine what is desirable and what is not. Once again we are brought back to the conclusion that we can carry on no useful discussion of the relation of evolution to progress unless we have a clearly formed conception of the standard of value by which we judge what progress is.

But, the biologist may rejoin, you may have your standard, but it is nugatory. Your conception of the goal of human endeavor may be clear enough, but in practice it may be futile. You desire a society based on mutual forbearance and mutual aid. But you cannot get it. The law of life is internecine struggle, and against that law you beat in vain. Well, let us accept this test and ask what we actually find. What we find is that the species which are from our point of view the higher, that is, those which exhibit the greater degree of individual development and social cooperation, come relatively late into existence in the course of evolution and tend to dominate the lower. Man, in whose development those characteristics are the most marked, is also the dominant animal and civilized societies which carry them farthest are dominant among mankind. The social type inherits the earth. It does not defeat itself. It succeeds.

These considerations necessarily have had their effect upon the biological view, and the conception of the struggle for existence has been modified accordingly. It is seen that, in dealing with social affairs, we cannot take the individual as an isolated unit, and the conception of competition is transferred accordingly from the individual human being to the social group of which he is a member. For this social group it is recognized that affection and sympathy, and all the forces that make for order and cooperation, will have what biologists term "survival value." Though inferior individuals may be preserved, for example, by the higher development of parental care, yet, upon the whole, the family in which parental love is strongest will have an advantage in competition with other families. It may contain a larger number of weak units, but, as a whole, it will have more solidarity and it will be better organized for the achievement of its ends.

As with the family, so with society. Each community will lose something by preservation of members who are ill-equipped, physically or morally, but it will gain more by its acceptance of those higher rules of social order and justice which prevent the stronger members from exercising their powers to the full.

But the gain in this method of treating the facts is still looked on as essentially a gain in competition. The struggle for existence is now conceived as a struggle between communities, and while it is admitted that in the community there is a certain suspension or mitigation of the war of all against all, it is insisted none the less that it is still through struggle, still through elimination, that progress takes place, only the elimination is now applied to communities as a whole; the weaker community goes under, and it is still well that it should go under.

So reconstituted, the theory affords justification for what is known in ethics as "group-morality." We are all familiar with the fact that a certain code may be generally recognized as applicable to all the members of a group, while outside that group quite another code comes into operation. The distinction of Greek and Barbarian, of Jew and Gentile, of white man and colored, are familiar illustrations. Here, again, it will be seen that the very modification of sentiment which before the days of biology was deemed to be the highest development of ethics, the change effected by overcoming these distinctions and forming a code of universalism in which there was to be neither Jew nor Gentile, bond nor free, is regarded by the theory of natural selection as a step to deterioration. Let our social principles be developed as highly as possible within the group, says the theory in its present form, but only on condition that between the groups themselves no terms of peace be made. Yet here, again, at bottom, our previous argument is once more applicable. For once again, if we look at history, if we consult the ethical consciousness to tell us what is higher, and if we verify its deliverance by tracing the results in the actual work of civilization, we find that the lowest stages of society are those in which men are organized in small, comparatively isolated groups; and as civilization advances we find processes of fusion at work whereby larger and better organized communities are formed and wherein the caste and class distinctions, which at first preserved the group organization, are more and more broken down. Just as in the ethics which we deem highest we find the barriers between man and man surmounted in principle, so in societies which we conceive as most highly civilized we find them in greater degree actually broken down by law and custom and practice of life.

Furthermore, the ideal of group-morality, as an ideal, is self-contradictory. We cannot deliberately and with our eyes open mutilate ethical principles and preserve the portion of them which we wish to cherish, unaffected by that operation. We cannot, for example, refuse the elementary rights of humanity to those who are not of our nation or race, and yet retain the conception of these rights in all their full, living vigor for use amongst ourselves. The obligations recognized under group-morality are never so complete as those which are founded on the conception of common morality. Nor lastly, can we justify aggressive war and conquest as methods of securing race-domination, without thereby laying our own social structure open to serious reactions. If we are to wage war, we must be organized as a military society. And this remark is general. Our own internal constitution is essentially correlated with our behavior to other communities. We cannot here escape the reaction of what we may, if we like, call moral laws or, if we prefer it, sociological effects. We cannot maintain one life, as it were, within, and another without.

The conclusion which these reflections suggest is that the uncritical application of biological principles to social progress results in an insuperable contradiction. The factors which determine the survival of physical organisms, if applied as rules for the furtherance of social progress, appear to conflict with all that social progress means. A sense of this conflict is no doubt responsible for the further reconstruction which the biological view has in recent years undergone. Biologists now begin to inquire seriously whether "natural" selection may not be replaced by a rational selection in which "fitness for survival" would at length achieve its legitimate meaning, and the development of the race might be guided by reasoned conceptions of social value. This is a fundamental change of attitude, and the new doctrine of eugenics to which it has given rise requires careful examination. Before proceeding to this examination, however, it will be well to inquire into the causes of the contrast on which we have insisted between biological evolution and social progress. Faced by this contradiction, we ask ourselves whether social development may not be something quite distinct from the organic changes known to biology, and whether the life of society may not depend upon forces which never appear in the individual when he is examined merely as an individual or merely as a member of a race.

Take the latter point first. It is easily seen in the arguments of biologists that they conceive social progress as consisting essentially in an improvement of the stock to which individuals belong. This is a way of looking at the matter intelligible enough in itself. Society consists of so many thousand or so many million individuals, and if, comparing any given generation with its ancestors, we could establish an average improvement in physical, mental, or moral faculty, we should certainly have cause to rejoice. There is progress so far. But there is another point of view which we may take up. Society consists of individual persons and nothing but individual persons, just as the body consists of cells and the product of cells. But though the body may consist exclusively of cells, we should never understand its life by examining the lives of each of its cells as a separate unit. We must equally take into account that organic interconnection whereby the living processes of each separate cell coöperate together to maintain the health of the organism which contains them all. So, again, to understand the social order we have to take into account, not only the individuals with their capabilities and achievements, but the social organization in virtue of which these individuals act upon one another and jointly produce what we call social results; and whatever may be true of the physical organism, we can see that in society it is possible that individuals of the very same potentialities may, with good organization, produce good results, and, with bad organization, results which are greatly inferior.[1]

The social phenomenon, in short, is not something which occurs in one individual, or even in several individuals taken severally. It is essentially an interaction of individuals, and as the capabilities of any given individual are extraordinarily various and are only called out, each by appropriate circumstances, it will be readily seen that the nature of the interaction may itself bring forth new and perhaps unexpected capacities, and elicit from the individuals contributing to it forces which, but for this particular opportunity, might possibly remain forever dormant. If this is so, sociology, as a science, is not the same thing as either biology or psychology. It deals neither with the physical capacities of individuals as such nor with their psychological capacities as such. It deals rather with results produced by the play of these forces upon one another, by the interaction of individuals under the conditions imposed by their physical environment. The nature of the forces and the point of these distinctions may be made clear by a very simple instance.

Let us picture to ourselves a crowd of persons trying to get through a narrow doorway. Here are a number of individuals, each animated by a common purpose. Let us consider the forces at work. Obviously, the first that we shall take into account is psychological — there

[1] It may be said that an improved organization must itself imply improvement of average individual quality. But this is not so. It may depend, *e.g.*, on contact with a higher civilization or on the successive efforts of generations of a stock which remains unmodified in its hereditary racial characteristics.

is the common motive to get out of the room animating every single component member of the crowd. Next come under consideration the biological elements — the strength of muscle, the soundness of wind and limb which enable each man to hold his place and push along. Then there are the physical conditions to be taken into account — the shape of the room, the width of the door. If the door were wide enough there would be no pushing; in other words, certain material limitations of the environment give form to the forces at work. Observe further that, under the general conditions laid down, the differences of individuals would have full play. One person goes intelligently in the line of least resistance; another makes his way through the crowd by the "infallible process" known to Mr. Alfred Jingle of elbowing the countenances of its component members; a third follows in the wake of some one stronger than himself; a fourth slips adroitly into every interstice that presents itself. Where in all this is the social phenomenon? It presents in this case no very dignified spectacle. It is just the boiling, seething, surging crowd and the process of its emergence as a whole, draggletailed and crushed it may be, from the scene of struggle. I ask you to note only that what has happened is something to be described neither in terms of the physical characteristics of the room, nor of the muscular strength of the individuals, nor of their psychological peculiarities, but in terms of the play of all these forces upon one another. The movement of the crowd is the result, not of a number of personal forces taken separately, but of a number of personal forces in interaction, and the interaction modifies the personal forces, bringing into play efforts which would not be made but for the situation which it creates.

Now, in this scene we had the social phenomenon at its lowest, as we know well from descriptions of what occurs when such a crash as I am picturing takes place under the influence of panic. But let us consider how the social phenomenon involved may be modified. Let us substitute a slightly different image. Instead of the crowd all animated by one purpose, anxious to pass in one direction, let us think of a busy London crossing. Here we have the same general conditions, with one modification to begin with, which makes the instance more appropriate as an example of social life at large. The people are not all going one way; they are not all animated by one motive; all want to get along, but they are going in different directions, and the crowds pass and repass. But what is still more important for our purpose, a new element has been introduced. The vehicles all keep on their side of the road, and at the crossing there stands a man in blue to show who may pass and who may not. By this simple means the multitudinous tumult of individual forces is reduced to a certain sufficiency of order, and this, on the one hand, by the unquestioning observance of a certain very simple custom and, on the other hand, by the presence of a representative of the majesty of the law — two methods by which in the course of ages society has solved for itself the problem of walking or driving along the street with the minimum of mutual hindrance. The two methods are those of custom on the one hand, and of the positive institution armed with authority upon the other. The orderly passage of the street is thus effected by people who, if placed under the conditions of panic or, for that matter, in a room from which they have to make their egress on the lines of our first demonstration, would have behaved very much in the way described. But if in the struggle of the crowd to get out of the room, some one man, with sufficient strength of voice or impressiveness of manner, should set himself to impose a little orderliness, we know how quickly a *queue* would be formed, and how the anarchic struggle of one minute would give way to a far more rapid and orderly egress in the next. We know too, how, if the conditions were repeated, the problem of maintaining order would in each successive instance become easier to solve.

Now, these instances, simple as they are, are typical of the life of society. They illustrate what is meant by the social fact as distinct from the biological and the psychological. They show that in sociology what we have to deal with is the results that come about from the interplay of motives, the behavior of men in the mass as they act and react upon one another. They show, secondly, how the very nature of this interaction will call forth new forces previously latent in the individuals concerned in the affair, and they show how the results so arrived at are incorporated in institutions. The interplay of human motives and the interaction of human beings is the fundamental fact of social life, and the permanent results which this interaction achieves and the influence which it exercises upon the individuals who take part in it, constitutes the fundamental fact of social evolution. These results are embodied in what may be called, generically, tradition. So understood, tradition, its growth and establishment, its reaction upon the very individuals who contribute to building it up, and its modifications by subsequent interactions, constitutes the main subject of sociological inquiry. Tradition is, in the development of society, what heredity is in the physical growth of the stock. It is the link between past and future, it is that in which the effects of the past are consolidated and on the basis of which subsequent modifications are built up. We might push the analogy a little further, for the ideas and customs which it maintains and furnishes to each new generation as guides for their behavior in life are analogous to the determinate methods of reaction, the inherited impulses, reflexes, and instincts with which heredity furnishes the individual. The tradition of the elders is, as it were, the instinct of society. It furnishes the prescribed rule for dealing with the ordinary occasions of life, which is for the most part accepted without inquiry and applied without reflection. It furnishes the appropriate institution for providing for each class of social needs, for meeting common dangers, for satisfying social wants, for regulating social relations. It constitutes, in short, the framework of society's life which to each new generation is a part of its hereditary outfit. But of course in speaking of tradition as a kind of inheritance we conceive of it as propagated by quite other than biological methods. In a sense its propagation is psychological, it is handed on from mind to mind, and even though social institutions may in a sense be actually incorporated in material things, in buildings, in books, in coronation robes, or in flags, still it need not be said that these things are nothing but for the continuity of thought which maintains and develops their significance. Yet the forces at work in tradition are not purely psychological; at least, they are not to be understood in terms of individual psychology alone. What is handed on is not merely a set of ideas, but the whole social environment; not merely certain ways of thinking or of acting, but the conditions which prescribe to individuals the necessity for thinking or acting in certain specific ways if they are to achieve their own desires. The point is worth dwelling on, because some writers have thought to simplify the working of tradition by reducing it to some apparently simple psychological phenomenon like that of imitation. In this there is more than one element of fallacy. To begin with, imitation itself is by no means a simple or unambiguous term. When we repeat what another does, we are not always imitating; when we learn from another, we are not always imitating. If the term is to be used strictly, it appears to be applicable to two main cases of repetition. In the simplest case, imitation appears as a kind of mechanical suggestion. Such, for example, is the case of contagious laughter or yawning; such is the case quoted by some psychologists of the smile of the mother mirrored almost automatically, as it would seem, on the face of the baby. Psychological contagion of this kind has its own sphere and its own importance in the life of society. It has its effect in the psychology of crowds and it has much to do with the more superficial movements of fashion. At a higher remove it becomes the desire to be as others are and do as others do, — a factor of course to be reckoned with, — along with which may be ranked the complementary impulse, to be what others are not, to differentiate oneself from the crowd.

These are the two types of imitation proper, the conscious and the unconscious, and both of them have an influence with which sociology has to reckon, but they are very far from exhausting the sphere of tradition. From any such imitative propagation of an idea or habit we must distinguish, as resting upon quite different psychological conditions, the propagation of ideas by teaching, by demonstration, and even by the appeal to the feelings and passions. The ultimate result may still in a sense be the same, — that is to say, the idea which is possessed by A passes into the mind of B, — but the method by which it is imparted and therefore the conditions under which it will spread from mind to mind are as different as need be. A much more complex psychology comes into play. No longer the simple desire of B to be like A, but the whole mental, and perhaps the whole social and physical, situation will have to be taken into account. B will accept the idea in so far as it will fit in with his mental predisposition, it may be with his feelings, it may be with his conceptions of logic, it may be with the requirements of the environment in which he finds himself. And finally, from all cases of the multiplication of an idea or a mode of action by passage from mind to mind, we must distinguish the multitudinous cases in which the same idea or the same mode of action is repeated over and over again, not because it is propagated from mind to mind, but because each individual mind finds itself similarly circumstanced. All the farmers in a countryside may be plowing their fields in the same week, not because they are imitating one another or are persuading one another, but because the requirements of their land are alike and the season is the same for all. And here, in the case of social institutions, we touch upon a factor which takes us outside the region of pure psychology, for what persists in social life is not merely the ideas which pass from mind to mind, but the whole fabric of society into which each man finds himself born and which in large measure determines the circumstances of his life, and the methods by which alone he can make his way in the world. To pursue the case of the farmer, for example, he plows his land, not merely in imitation of his father, but because by certain laws of inheritance the land has become his in virtue of his sonship, and to work it is just the method which the social fabric provides for him to obtain his living. In other words, tradition not merely supplies him with certain ideas of what he may do, but fixes him in a position in which it is open to him to do certain things and not others.

Now, the growth of tradition will in a sense gravely modify the individual members of the society which maintains it. To any given set of institutions a certain assemblage of qualities, mental and physical, will be most appropriate, and these may differ as much as the qualities necessary for war differ from those of peaceful industry. Any tradition will obviously call forth from human beings the qualities appropriate to it, and it will in a sense select the individuals in which those qualities are the best developed and will tend to bring them to the top of the social fabric, but this is not to say that it will assert the same modification upon the stock that would be accomplished by the working of heredity. The hereditary qualities of the race may remain the same, though the traditions have changed and though by them one set of qualities are kept permanently in abeyance, while the other are continually brought by exercise to the highest point of efficiency. According to the prevailing views of heredity, no amount of such exercise, however long repeated, would affect those innate characteristics of the stock which are handed on from parent to child, and thus it is conceivable that we might find very great social advances in any given direction without any modification of the inherited characteristics of the race. We are not to conclude that physical heredity is of no importance to the social order; it must be obvious that the better the qualities of the individuals constituting a race, the more easily they will fit themselves into good social traditions, the more readily they will advance those traditions to a still higher point of excellence, and the more stoutly they would resist deterioration. The qualities upon which the social fabric calls must be there, and the more readily they are forthcoming the more easily the social machine will work. Hence social progress necessarily implies a certain level of racial development, and its advance may always be checked by the limitations of the racial type. Nevertheless, if we look at human history as a whole, we are impressed with the stability of the great fundamental characteristics of human nature and the relatively sweeping character and often rapid development of social change. In view of this contrast we must hesitate to attribute any substantial share in human development to biological factors, and our hesitation is increased when we consider the factors on which social change depends.

It is in the department of knowledge and industry that advance is most rapid and certain, and the reason is perfectly clear. It is that on this side each generation can build on the work of its predecessors. A man of very moderate mathematical capacity to-day can solve problems which puzzled Newton, because he has available the work of Newton and of many another since Newton's time. In the department of ethics the case is different. Each man's character has to be formed anew, and though teaching goes for much, it is not everything. The individual in the end works out his own salvation. Where there is true ethical progress is in the advance of ethical conceptions and principles which can be handed on; of laws and institutions which can be built up, maintained, and improved. That is to say, there is progress just where the factor of social tradition comes into play and just so far as its influence extends. If the tradition is broken, the race begins again where it stood before the tradition was formed. We may infer that while the race has been relatively stagnant, society has rapidly developed, and we must conclude that, whether for good or for evil, social changes are mainly determined, not by alterations of racial type, but by modifications of tradition due to the interactions of social causes. Progress is not racial, but social.

CHAPTER III

THE VALUE AND LIMITATIONS OF EUGENICS

WE have seen that social life consists in the interaction of human beings, and social evolution — whether progressive or the reverse — in the consequent formation and modification of what, for lack of a better single word, we may call the social tradition. Social improvement therefore is not the same as racial improvement. It is quite conceivable that with no change in the average level of racial capacity, the cumulative efforts of generations to better their life might produce a very great change in the social structure, and in point of fact it appears to be mainly by such a process of the summation of effort that the actual achievements of mankind have been effected. But at this point the biological critic may very fairly break in with a new criticism. "Granted," he may say, "all that you urge on behalf of the social tradition. It still remains the incontestable truth that society is composed of individuals whose qualities determine the nature of their interactions. No doubt these qualities are very complex. Man is a being of mixed disposition. There is a mingling of gold and brass in every soul, and circumstances may decide which is to show on the surface. We grant then that there are wide limits of variation within which, without modification of the racial type, society may advance or retrograde. None the less we

VALUE AND LIMITATIONS OF EUGENICS

come back to the qualities of individuals as the ultimate determinants. Their average merit must affect the standard of social action. Conceive the racial level — by which we mean the average level of hereditary endowment — raised, and to that extent you facilitate social progress. Conceive it lowered, and to that extent you arrest progress and favor deterioration." The contention thus modestly put cannot be denied. The very efforts that men make to improve their individual condition and the social order are themselves of course the outcome of their qualities; and if these qualities take shape and find expression in the medium of the social tradition, it is equally true that they form the ultimate reserve of energy underlying the social changes by which that tradition is maintained, improved, or destroyed "Very well then," the Eugenist proceeds, "it is admitted that the quality of the stock is of high importance. It is admitted also that natural selection is no longer capable of performing its function in weeding out inferior stocks. It is admitted that we cannot revert to the use of natural selection without destroying the characteristic work of civilization. We cannot undo the structure of mutual aid and mutual forbearance which civilized progress has painfully built up. What we can do is to substitute for natural a rational selection. We may discourage and even prevent the perpetuation of inferior stocks, and for this purpose a rational conception of fitness and a knowledge of the laws of heredity is all that we require. All that has been urged above against the conception of the struggle for existence may be true. It holds true none the less that selection is necessary to racial progress and to the avoidance of racial deterioration, and even if the social reformer could ignore the need of improvement in the race, he must take a very serious view of the possibilities involved in deterioration. He must look very carefully at the reforms which he is proposing, for fear any such vital injury to the life-blood of society should be entailed by them."

Without examining all the details of this argument, we may admit the main contention to be theoretically sound. The improvement of the stock by rational selection is in the abstract a clearly legitimate object. It involves no such contradiction with the inherent trend of progress as is contained in the principle of leaving society to the operation of the unchecked struggle for existence. The child once born has a claim upon society which can only be ignored at the cost of abandoning the basic principles of the humanized social order. But the claim to bring children into the world is quite another matter. It is no novel point of ethics to forbid parentage to a person of deeply vitiated stock, and Eugenists who draw a distinction between the right to live and the right to bring to life are within their rights. So far then we admit that the eugenic conclusion follows from its premises. But what are the premises? We are to assume, first, that we have a true conception of social worth, of the nature of human progress and of the qualities making for it. We are to assume, secondly, that we have competent knowledge of the laws of inheritance whereby we can so play upon the race as to engender the qualities that we desire. This is, to succeed in eugenics we need a competent understanding both of the eu and of the genics. We

VALUE AND LIMITATIONS OF EUGENICS

must know what we want to breed for and how we propose to breed for it. Have we the clearness of conception as to the first point and the fullness of knowledge as to the second which are necessary to the useful development of eugenics?

As to the first question, the nature and criterion of social worth, I think we may trace two lines of thought among eugenic writers which it is highly important to distinguish. The more careful admit that for a thoroughgoing application of their principle we should need a well-grounded social philosophy. They admit that little is known as to the causation of many of the higher human qualities and fully grant that we should be very careful in, so as to say, passing sentence of execution on a stock which may after all contain serviceable elements mixed with its blemishes. But they say there are many qualities about which there can be no doubt. We do not want insanity; we do not want feeble-mindedness; we do not want alcoholism; we do not want syphilis; we do not want the stocks which are infected with such taint. We want to extinguish them as evil in themselves and as liable to infect sound stocks. We want to isolate those definitely infected much as we isolate an infectious disease. We want to prevent them from bringing into the world children in their own image. When the principle is admitted and the experiment has been made in these cases that are clear, it will be time enough to consider those that are more doubtful. We shall in the meantime have gained some knowledge of what can be done by these means and how it can be done with the least possible infliction of suffering.

On this side we see the eugenic case at its strongest. But even here we must put in one caveat. There may be blemishes which are very serious in themselves, but which nevertheless do not afford adequate grounds for pronouncing capital sentence upon a stock. As an illustration, I will take the case of tuberculosis. The heredity of this disease is still a matter of some question. For the sake of argument I will assume the diathesis to be hereditary. No one can deny that it is in that case a serious blemish. But before we proceeded to pass sentence of exclusion from the rights of parenthood on any individual of tubercular stock, I think we should have very carefully to weigh two questions. The first is, what are the other qualities of the individual? Liability to tubercular infection involves no mental or moral turpitude. It may coexist with the highest qualities on this side. I am not aware that it even involves any other form of physical weakness, though some other forms of physical weakness may no doubt increase the liability to tubercular infection. Now, if we stamp out the tubercular tendency, what other qualities are we stamping out along with it? If an otherwise gifted stock has this blemish, will there be net loss or net gain in its disappearance? I do not think that this question can be answered offhand. But if our general view of progress is correct, society has on the whole gone forward by the development of those arts which assist to keep alive many who without such aid would have perished; and considering the very wide prevalence which is now believed to obtain of some form or another of the tubercular condition, it may be doubted, whether if the tubercle had been left to

VALUE AND LIMITATIONS OF EUGENICS 45

do its work unchecked, there would have been any social progress at all. Secondly, it is well within the bounds of possibility that, by the development of scientific hygiene, instead of eliminating the tubercular stock we may succeed in eliminating the tubercle. In that case this particular tendency — unless provably correlated with some other form of irremediable weakness — will no longer rank as a defect. If in the meantime we had prohibited the marriage of members of such stocks, we should have lost all that they might have contributed to the population and its well-being for the sake of no permanent gain.

These two points may be stated generally. We must be certain that the stock which we seek to eliminate is so vicious that its removal is a net gain. We must be sure that the vice is irremovable and not dependent upon conditions which it is within our power to modify. This latter condition implies a certainty as to the operation of heredity, of which more will be said. But meanwhile, assuming those two conditions fulfilled, there is a case for forbidding parentage — always upon this further provision that in so doing we do not allow ourselves to be driven to methods which by violating the painfully acquired traditions of civilization will aid the ever present tendencies to re-barbarization. On these grounds the case of the feeble-minded becomes perhaps the strongest for the application of eugenic methods. We have here a type which it is becoming possible to identify with fair precision. It is found in men and women who are not capable of independent existence, but who continually drift to the gaol or the workhouse, who are fertile, and whose condition is asserted to be hereditary in a marked degree. On grounds of humanity we have good reason to undertake the care of this class, and we have a right to demand in return the separation of the sexes. We are dealing with people who are not capable of guiding their own lives and who should for their own sake be under tutelage, and we are entitled to impose our own conditions of this tutelage, having the general welfare of society in view. Lastly, there is no reason to think that this condition is an isolated and, as it were, accidental defect in a nature that is otherwise healthy and sound. The evidence, I understand, is rather that it is a form of general deterioration not correlated with any specially good qualities by way of compensation. Such a case is, I think, one of the strongest that Eugenists can press in the present state of our knowledge.

On such lines as these, physiological or medical lines as we may call them, eugenics may have a part to play in relation to the social problem. But meanwhile there is a second line of thought discernible among Eugenists and larger claims put forward bearing on political thought as a whole which must be very carefully scrutinized. By no means all eugenic writers are so careful in their application of the tests of unfitness as those to whom I have referred. To read a good deal of what is written on this subject one might suppose that the whole question is as simple as daylight. Often it would seem as if the actual position of classes in society was taken as a measure of their worth. Thus we hear a great deal of the relative sterility of the richer classes and the fertility of the poorer, as if this were in

VALUE AND LIMITATIONS OF EUGENICS 47

itself sufficient evidence of the multiplication of the unfit. Now, the actual forces which determine a man's position in modern society are, first, the inheritance of property and other social privileges, and secondly, his capacity for making and keeping money. The first of these, far from affording a test of personal merit, tends to mask the actual inequalities of endowment. One knows people of the essential pauper character in all classes. But whereas if they are born among the well-to-do they exist on means of their own or find relations on whom they succeed in fastening, among the poor they drift to the street corner, the casual ward, the workhouse, and the gaol. One would suppose it axiomatic that without perfect equality of opportunity actual position in the social scale would be no criterion of relative merit; and yet we find at least one able writer so enamoured of the qualities of the British upper and middle class that he manages on eugenic grounds to find reasons for the maintenance of class distinctions. But further, given a genuine freedom of competition and full equality of opportunity, the qualities which bring men to the top are not necessarily social qualities. Some qualities by which men get on are good, some indifferent, and some bad. Which of these will predominate depends on the character of the social organization. The financial abilities which bring men to the top to-day may come to be regarded by our descendants much as we regard the qualities of a robber baron who prospered under mediæval conditions. Upon the whole it is probable that the harder and more self-regarding qualities still play a larger part than the gentler and more social in determining success, and we are not surprised when we find writers of the type to which I refer telling us plainly that self-reliance and endurance are the qualities which they wish to breed. Now, self-reliance and endurance are very good qualities, and we must not depreciate them, but a view of human nature which centers on these to the omission of the other side of character is a view which has got out of focus. The possibility of such a view indicates the absolute necessity of a social philosophy as a basis of eugenics the moment that eugenic considerations are used to determine the main lines of social reform.

In fact, when they begin to criticize social reform, some Eugenists of the class to which I am referring, political Eugenists as we may call them, come perilously near to the old arguments from the theory of natural selection. They make reservations, it is true, which must stand to their credit. They admit that the social conscience is an indispensable factor in progress, and that what has been done in the way of ameliorative legislation cannot be undone. But, they argue, as long as natural selection reigned the standard of the stock was kept up. The weakling was eliminated; the strong survived. Now natural selection is superseded. The weakling is preserved. He is allowed to breed. Relatively he is more fertile than the fit. The birth-rate diminishes most among the higher ranks of society. More and more the nation of the future will be recruited from the unfit stocks. Meanwhile the burden of maintaining the unfit falls in the shape of poor rates and state taxes on the shoulders of their betters, who are thus positively handicapped in the struggle and disinclined to rear families. All social legislation is directed to the improvement of the environment, but the improvement of the environment has no effect on the stock. It may in some degree — Professor Pearson's school argues that it is in a very slight degree — improve the qualities of the individual, but the qualities so acquired will not be handed on. Unless we so alter our institutions as to encourage the propagation of the fit and discourage the unfit, our race is doomed.

(1) If these jeremiads were well founded, we should expect to see the signs of deterioration already manifest. After all, the suspension of natural selection is no new phenomenon. It has, as we have shown, been in progress ever since civilization began and even before civilization began. True, with the decline of the infantile death rate it has been carried much farther, but this is only the continuance of a very old process, and that this process can ever go so far as entirely to eliminate natural selection is unlikely. Variations which are sufficiently extreme are likely always to carry early death or infertility as their effect. In our own times what proof is there of actual deterioration? As it happens a committee was instituted in my own country to investigate this question some six years ago. There was at that time a widespread uneasiness arising from the increasing number of recruits who were rejected on medical grounds. Physical deterioration was the thing most feared, and it was reasonable to suppose that under modern considerations it would be on this side if anywhere that deterioration would be apparent. The committee was not biased in favor of any optimistic view, and all available evidence in favor of deterioration came before them. The result was

that while they found that there was no sufficient material as at present available to warrant any definite conclusions on the question of the physique of the people by comparison with data obtained in past times, yet "the impressions gathered from the great majority of the witnesses examined do not support the belief that there is any general progressive physical deterioration." Familiar social statistics support the negative view. The heavy decline of the death-rate during the last forty years is undoubtedly due to improved sanitary and social conditions, but it also indicates an improvement of general health, and if there were any strong tendency to the deterioration of the stock at work, we should expect it to appear as at least a counterpoise. The decline of pauperism from about 50 per thousand of the population in 1850 to 21 per thousand in the present year is also due to general social progress; but it has gone on long enough to be seriously counteracted by the growth of a class of hereditary paupers, supposing that such a class were in fact increasing. Of the diminution of crime in proportion to the population — which, notwithstanding a recent rise, marks the period as a whole — the same may be said. Lastly, the rise in real wages, which is slow but general in England and is spread over a century, tells the same tale. Wages have risen owing to a variety of social efforts, but the higher wage could hardly in the competition of the world's market be earned by a continuously deteriorating population of workers. The only unfavorable comparison of any weight that can be instituted with the past is in the matter of insanity, and here the interpretation of the figures is subject to serious doubt.

There is, says the committee, in the report which I have quoted, no doubt as to the great increase of insane persons under treatment, but the question is, first, how far these figures indicate true increase of insanity, and secondly, if this is true, as to the causes of the increase. On the first point they rely chiefly on the evidence of Dr. Wiglesworth, who, they say, admitted that the statistical information was incomplete, and that the conclusions to be drawn from it varied according as it was read and looked at, but on the whole, though he would like to express himself with reserve, was inclined to think that the incidence was increasing. You see how cautiously the opinion as to the last fact is expressed. When we come to the interpretation, we find Dr. Wiglesworth equally cautious as to the argument that the increase of lunacy can be taken as evidence of physical deterioration. So far as England is concerned it appears to be connected with density of population, and therefore, if it is real, to be rather an effect of the worst side of the social environment — the crush and the strain of industrial life — than of deterioration of stock.[1] Upon the whole we are justified in the conclusion that whatever the future has in store the process of deterioration has not begun.

(2) In the absence of inductive evidence of race deterioration, we may usefully go on to inquire whether there is any reason in the nature of the case why the suspension of natural selection within the limits up to which such suspension is possible should lower

[1] There is in fact more evidence of the increase of lunacy in Ireland, which has for historical reasons failed in large measure to share in such social progress as the larger island has achieved.

the racial standard. To many biologists the question refutes itself. The race is forever varying, but its variations for the worse are nipped in the bud. Once allow them to grow and they must infect the sounder stocks. At a minimum they must lower the racial average, and this process of deterioration will go on indefinitely. It is by means of the selection of small variations for the better that the racial standard is improved and that new varieties and new species are formed. Similarly, by the indefinitely continued propagation of variations for the worse, the whole standard of a race will be lowered. This large way of looking at the facts, however, implies a biological theory which is by no means universally accepted. How far a race is actually capable of being modified by the accumulation of small variations has become in recent years a matter of acute controversy, and it seems to be the better opinion that a distinction must be drawn between the less important variations known as fluctuations and the more deep-seated changes to which the name of mutations has been given. It is probable that in the case of smaller fluctuations there is a constant tendency to return to the mean or standard of the race, and if we can imagine a race wholly immune from natural selection and not striking out any new line by a definite mutation, the mean standard of the racial type would be roughly maintained for an indefinite period. But be that as it may, we have to point out once more that the view taken of the effect of natural selection is one-sided, for once again it is assumed that it is only the unfit who are eliminated. Now if once for all we get rid of the phrase "selection of the fit" and substitute for it "elimination of the unsuccessful," which is what is really meant, we shall see the facts in a different light. In a race subject to a severe struggle for existence, the types which are unsuccessful under the prevailing conditions will constantly be eliminated; but it is possible and more than possible that these types should include among them the most valuable stocks for the purposes of society. Where the conditions of life are hard, where there is little regard for justice and mercy, and in a word for all the higher ethical qualities, those who possess these qualities have less chance of prospering and leaving descendants behind them. In point of fact in earlier forms of human society there is good reason to think that social progress was seriously interfered with by the actual elimination of the best types. From this point of view political and civil liberty, social and economic justice, are the most eugenic of agencies. Much is said by Eugenists of the decay of nations in the past by the failure of the best types to perpetuate themselves. I know of no case, not even that of the Roman Empire, in which this suggestion is susceptible of any clear historical proof, for the lamentations over the decay of the Roman population date from the first century before Christ, a period which history has shown to have been, not one of retrogression, but of progress,—a progress which was well maintained for two centuries after the time when these jeremiads had become familar. It is also forgotten by those who make use of the half-told tale of Roman decadence that, as the Roman Empire consolidated itself, it drew for its support, not on the old aristocracy of Rome, but on the newer population of the Mediterranean basin, and that this population was decadent or was seriously affected by the relatively fast multiplication of inferior stocks is a suggestion for which I have never seen any evidence. On the other hand, if we look at the artificial elimination of the best stocks by political and religious despotism, we get much more definite evidence of national deterioration. Take, for example, the case of Spain in the sixteenth century. We need not assume that the Protestant reformers were man for man better than the old believers; but we may fairly suppose that a large proportion of the more independent minds and more active thinkers would be attracted by the new creed, and when we find that these were eliminated by the process of *auto da fé* to the number of tens of thousands, we can well understand that in Spain the selection effected by political circumstances may have been such as to denude the country of an undue proportion of its most vigorous stocks. Speaking broadly, if the more social qualities are to have their chance, it is on political and social institutions that that chance must depend. Freedom of thought and action, freedom of choice by women, the repression of violence and fraud, these are all eugenic agencies which tend to diminish the contrast between the successful and the fit. So regarded, the improvement of social conditions is seen to tell both ways in its effect on the stock. If it admits of variations for the bad, it also allows for variations for the good. So far the two tendencies cancel one another. But we may go a step farther. The actual progress of humanity depends far more on the survival of the best than on the elimination of the worst; provided that the highest types can always have breathing space, we may be assured that social, as distinct from racial, progress will continue. Eugenically considered then, the broad duty of society is so to arrange its institutions that success is to the socially fit, and this is only possible in proportion as the social order is based on principles of a just and equitable organization.

(3) In this account of the matter I have assumed, in accordance with the preponderance of biological opinion, that environment as such has no direct effect upon the development of the stock. This is a point on which some schools of biologists speak with an assurance which almost amounts to dogmatism, and they employ this principle as an argument to prove the futility of contemporary efforts at social improvement. In so doing it may be remarked in passing that very frequently they fail to draw the necessary distinction between racial and social progress. Thus in one of the Eugenics Laboratory Lectures [1] we read: —

"Practically all social legislation has been based on the assumption that better environment meant race progress."

I beg leave to doubt whether for the most part persons interested in social legislation have given any profound consideration to the question of race progress. What they have been concerned with is social progress, that is to say, they have aimed at improving the actual life of the people and the building up of a better social structure, and I may add that the biological terms of race and environment, nature and nurture, are not cate-

[1] "The Relative Strength of Nurture and Nature," by Ethel M. Elderton.

gories to satisfy sociologists. They do not exhaust the field. From one point of view, no doubt, social institutions may be regarded as an environment within which the individual is formed and to which he has to accommodate himself. But the actual effect of social institutions upon life is not to be understood in biological terms. The relation, as Professor Henry Jones has well pointed out, between the individual and society is far more intimate. It is much more like an organic union. One and the same set of qualities will take a totally different expression according as the social environment differs. The very same motives, the same original characteristics, which will in the one set of circumstances lead a man to unsocial practices, will, if suitably directed, render him an efficient and useful citizen. The same motives of pride and self-assertion which in a land where the blood feud reigns would lead a man to decorate his home with the skulls of his enemies and their wives and children, will in a civilized society urge him on to commercial or professional success, and will compel him to serve society for the gratification of his own ambition. The necessity of earning a living will impel a man to robbery and fraud or to honest and useful labor in accordance with the opportunities which the social system holds out to him. The driving power which under unrestrained competition will make a man a hard master may under suitable social control be directed to the equally efficient and humane conduct of business. It is not human quality, whether original or acquired, that differs profoundly from period to period. It is the turn given to human quality by the social structure. As with the self-regarding, so with the more generous impulses. The unreasoned philanthropy of an earlier time might do harm by indiscriminate giving; when it finds rational channels for its activity it will prompt a man to throw in his weight with the best civic movements of the day. Nor, again, is the effect of social institutions to be measured by modifications in the qualities of individuals as that expression would be generally understood. Take, for example, the effect of education. It is certainly desirable that education should develop the intelligence, but how much net addition is made to intellectual capacity by educational processes is exceedingly difficult to measure. Acquired knowledge or skill, on the other hand, are tangible achievements in which the response of the individual on the one side and the teaching provided on the other are two inseparable conditions. It is acquirement or achievement, *e.g.* knowledge, skill, discipline, that training confers, and the modifications thus effected in a man's life and his functions as a member of society are so great as to amount in many cases to a change of kind rather than of degree. The distinction is ignored by certain writers of the eugenic school, who seek to depreciate the effect of nurture as compared with nature, even in its bearing on the individual. But apart from this some of the methods used to measure the effect of the environment are of very doubtful value. Thus, in the lecture already quoted, Miss Elderton seeks to measure the effect of the environment by utilizing the Report of the Charity Organization Society on certain school children in Edinburgh. The home environment of the children is considered under the following heads : —

The number of people per room;
Good economic conditions;
Good physical condition of parents;
Good moral condition of parents.

With regard to the last point, Miss Elderton admits there is room for variation of judgment, and one would say that even the three former would require very close investigation in order to form an accurate classification. However, having made this classification, Miss Elderton proceeds to take the reports on certain qualities of the children, on their vision, hearing, glandular condition, and intelligence; on some of these points I confess I should not expect the environment to produce any very marked effect, but the question of intelligence is interesting from our point of view, and here Miss Elderton is able to produce results indicating in her opinion a very small, if not a negligible, effect. Good economic conditions alone show a small influence upon the intelligence alike of boys and girls.[1] On these figures it must be remarked that they include

---

[1] The actual correlations are as follows: —

	Boys	Girls
Number of people per room (intelligence)	.02	.04
Good economic conditions (intelligence)	.01	.16
Good physical condition of parents (intelligence)	−.04	.06
Good moral condition of parents (intelligence)	−.07	.03

The negative signs indicate that the better conditions are associated with lower intelligence. The insignificance of the figures is to be measured by the fact that the general figure of correlation for heredity is taken by the writer to be about .49 in the case of intelligence.

several doubtful and even unknown quantities. How is the intelligence of boys and girls measured? On this vital point we have no information. At best it represents some impression of somebody, presumably of teachers, and what sort of standard is applied by which the fractions are determined we are not told. But if we take the figures at their face value, we find an exceedingly paradoxical result. It is constantly assumed that better economic and social conditions are generally indicative of superiority of stock. In that case the parents conforming to the better conditions are, it is to be inferred, men and women of better stock; and according to this, apart altogether from environmental influences, we should expect their children to show better results. We should expect the full correlation worked out for us in other cases of heredity. How is it that this fails when the present test is applied? We seem driven to the conclusion either that this particular method of calculation is misleading or that the general assumption upon which many of the sociological arguments of Eugenists are based, that the socially more fortunate classes are of the best hereditary strain, is unfounded. It must be added that when the home conditions are used as a test of the general effect of the environment, some very serious omissions are made. It appears to be forgotten that in a great measure the environment of all the children attending the same school, or even schools of the same class in a single town, is identical, particularly as regards the effect on intelligence. The school teaching is identical for all, and beyond that, all the children are born in the same area, in the same town, under the same law, and have to conform to the same standard of civilization; they learn the same things and are accessible to the same ideas. We get nothing but a fractional measure of the environment when we merely differentiate home surroundings.

Lastly, it will be seen that the writer does not even take in home surroundings as a whole. She divides them into heads and under each head finds a correlation which is very small compared with that of physical heredity. Now, if the comparison were to denote anything at all, it must begin by attempting to set the whole of the environmental conditions on the one side against the whole of hereditary conditions on the other. To take one environmental condition among many and to compare its effect with the total effect of physical heredity is a method of argument which can throw no light on the question at issue, and to take several environmental conditions in series without attempting to sum their effect is to produce an illusion of proof without reality.

An illustration equally remarkable in its own way of the mental processes by which some eugenic writers arrive at conclusions which go out to the public as the ordinances of the scientific world may be found in another publication of the same laboratory on "The Inheritance of Vision." The writers, Miss Amy Barrington and Professor Pearson, in summarizing their conclusion begin by remarking that it is "admittedly only a first study." "No one can recognize its defects more fully than the authors themselves do." With this becomnig modesty they go on to speak of the difficulties of obtaining evidence and then remark that as far as "the admittedly slender data of this first study " allow certain specific conclusions may be formulated which they then state in a manner to which no objection can be taken. Having stated them, they proceed to speak in more general terms.

"As far as the material developed in this memoir goes, it points, if not overwhelmingly, at least strongly, to the moral: Pay attention to breeding, and the environmental element will not affect your projects. Improve to the utmost your environment, breeding will lay low your schemes.

"The first thing is good stock, and the second thing is good stock, and the third thing is good stock, and when you have paid attention to these three things, fit environment will keep your material in good condition. No environmental or educational grindstone is of service, unless the tool to be ground is of genuine steel — of tough race and tempered stock.

"To bring home this fact in each department of human physique and mentality seems to be the urgent social problem of to-day."

This is a somewhat rapid transition from the cautious and scientific to the dogmatizing mood. The conclusions from "admittedly slender data" are first made to suggest a general conclusion which goes far beyond the particular case investigated. In the next paragraph the conclusion is dogmatically asserted without the least reference to the slenderness of the evidence, and in the third it has become the basis of practical statesmanship and to drive it home the most urgent social problem of the day. And this goes forth to the world as the decisive word of true science with its caution, its detachment, its objectivity, its reasonableness.

We may lay down with some confidence, first, that, as to the relative effect of nature and nurture upon the individual, no adequate means of measurement have yet been suggested; and secondly, that it is not the modification of the inherent qualities of the individual that is alone to be regarded, but the actual life to be lived by the individual in society, and that means, when all individuals are considered, the total character of the social fabric. Lastly, we must ask whether, in a sober review of our biological knowledge, the effect of the environment can be so completely dismissed as some biologists suppose. The more cautious adherents of the school of Weismann are careful to distinguish two separate questions. The first is whether any distinct quality impressed upon the individual is likely to be perpetuated in the stock. This they answer with a negative, not strictly upon the ground that such perpetuation has in all cases been actually disproved, but rather because no positive evidence is forthcoming of any such effect, nor has any method been shown by which it could be brought about; but they point out that this is not to settle the further question whether the environment may so influence the organism as a whole as to produce some effect upon the germ. Thus Professor Thomson writes [1] of the possibility that the germ-plasm should be "affected along with the body by a deeply saturating influence, which nobody has ever denied. The influence of toxins, for example, on the germ-plasm is in certain cases definitely admitted." Again [2] "it is generally admitted that when parents have healthy occupations their offspring are likely to be more vigorous. The matter is complicated by the difficulty of estimating how much is due to good nurture

[1] p. 187.   [2] *Ibid.*, p. 190.

VALUE AND LIMITATIONS OF EUGENICS 63

before and after birth. It is not unlikely, too, that some profound parental modifications may influence the general constitution, may even affect the germ-cells and may thus have results in the offspring, but unless the offspring show peculiarities in the same direction as the original modifications, we have no data bearing precisely on the question at issue." The question at issue is how the rise of specific qualities in the individual corresponds to impressed qualities in the parents. The passage indicates that there may be a broad and general effect where there is no specific effect.

Now when we are considering the purely biological problem of the way in which new species are formed, the question whether specific acquired characteristics are hereditary is of the first importance. But when, as sociologists, we are considering whether on the whole a healthy environment is likely to affect the germ-plasms favorably and an unhealthy environment unfavorably, we are dealing with a matter of equal practical importance, which is not to be determined by a negative answer to the previous question. We should certainly be risking a good deal if, in the present stage of our biological knowledge, we were to proceed on the assumption that no degree of unhealthiness in the conditions of life would have any permanent tendency to deterioration, and here, from the sociological point of view, the effect upon the mother would be just as important as the effect upon the germ-plasm. The biologist tends to rule out this consideration because from the moment the embryo is formed the effect upon the germ-plasm is no longer in question, but on the practical side the indirect influences upon the unborn child are just as important as the influences on the germinal cells which go to constitute the child. It must be added that all careful students of heredity admit the plenitude of our ignorance as to variation and that there are not wanting indications that the environment has indirect and subtle effects which have yet to be measured. We shall have to know more of the response of racial types to new surroundings and of the mechanism by which this response is effected before we can be sure that, not indeed by the direct transmission of acquired characters, but by some far more subtle series of spontaneous responses to new stimuli, the race does not adapt itself, as a race, to changed conditions, whether for good or ill.

(4) Nevertheless, we are told that the multiplication of inferior stocks and the relative infertility of the best is a serious feature of the social life of our day. What are the facts upon which this warning is based? In Professor Pearson's lecture on "The Problem of Practical Eugenics" we find a table comparing the fertility in pathological and in normal stocks. The pathological stock consists of deaf-mutes, English and American, tuberculous, albinotic, insane stocks, Edinburgh degenerates, London and Manchester mentally defective, and criminals. The mean size of the family for all these stocks is 6.2. With these are compared a series composed as follows: the English middle class; family records (presumably English); English intellectual class; working class, New South Wales; Danish professional class; Danish working class; Edinburgh normal artisan, and London normal artisan; and the mean of these is 5.5. The difference as it stands is not so

very alarming. We have to remark that the working classes of New South Wales and the professional and working classes of Denmark are not properly to be compared with classes of the British population, and that these tend to pull down the average. More serious, perhaps, are the figures which indicate a very low fertility in the two classes which Professor Pearson adds of English intellectuals, for which the normal size of the family, as given by Mr. Sidney Webb's results, is stated to be only 1.5, and of Harvard graduates, for which the corresponding figure is 2.0. Putting aside altogether the question of the test of fitness and assuming that, for the sake of argument, we have here some proof that the class that we should wish to see multiplied is relatively infertile, we must ask how far this result is due to social causes, and to what sort of social causes it is to be attributed. Biologists are familiar with the general law, first formulated by Herbert Spencer, that individual development and fertility vary inversely; right through the scale of creation the higher type reproduces itself in smaller numbers, and it seems to remain true among human beings that the race is upon the whole recruited in larger numbers from the normal and perhaps even from the lower types than from the higher. Is there any reason to think that this is a new phenomenon in the history of human development? If not, we can say that, though it is a regrettable fact, humanity has progressed in spite of it and that this would be only one sign among others of the general truth of the view that human progress is social and not racial. But are there not new facts to be taken into account? One there certainly is. It is the new opportunities opened by modern

society to women for other careers than that of the wife
and mother. There is the increased consideration of the
more thoughtful men for the health of their wives and
of the more thoughtful men and women for the up-
bringing of their children. These considerations, rather
than the selfishness to which it is commonly imputed,
are the principal causes of the limitation of the family
among more civilized peoples. It is reasonable that
these considerations, just as they are in themselves,
should be balanced by a longer and larger view of the
necessities of the race, and it is probable that, so far as
the restrictive tendency has gone beyond what is actually necessary for healthy conditions, the general recognition of this fact would tend to correct it. Just as
we saw in an earlier lecture that the Malthusian teaching had tended to lower the general rate of reproduction,
so, in response to a widely diffused belief that the quality of the race might be injuriously affected by the refusal of the best individuals to contribute to it, what is
excessive in the tendency would correct itself. So far
the Eugenist is within his rights in calling attention to
the dwindling of the family among the more educated
classes. He is wrong only if he insists on quantitative
reproduction at the expense of qualitative life, if he re-
turns to the conception of woman as limited in her
function to the bearing and rearing of children, and
omits from consideration the fact that the production
of a capable stock at the expense of the permanent
sacrifice of all that is most desirable in the life of one
half of it, is not an intelligible or self-consistent ideal.
He is wrong again when he overlooks the increased
sense of parental responsibility which, gradually spread-

ing through all classes of the population, expresses itself in the view that it is wrong to bring children into the world for whom no adequate provision can be made. He is wrong, in short, if he does not seek to bring his biological requirement into conformity with sociological conditions. It must be added that, so far as economic conditions affect the birth-rate in different classes, a very careful analysis is necessary to determine what precisely these economic conditions are. The limitation of the family among the more educated classes has no connection with the social legislation designed to ameliorate the social conditions of the poor. On this point those who have made no first-hand study of economics are apt too readily to take up the cry of the burden of the rates, and to accept the view that the middle classes are staggering under the load imposed on them by provision for the poor. This view of the incidence of taxation will not bear criticism. I must not here attempt a detailed investigation, but it may be shown in the first place that the total provision for the poorer classes in my own country in the matter of education, poor rate, old age pensions, and all the rest combined is but a fraction of the total national expenditure, and bears a quite insignificant relation to the actual income of the middle and upper classes. It may be shown, moreover, that of the burden of the rates a great part, even under our present system, falls not upon the occupier, who makes the direct payment, but upon owners who in the main are much too wealthy to be affected in their capacity of fathers of families thereby. And it may be shown, lastly, that by revised forms of rating and taxation no burden need be thrown upon any producer, nor need any single human being be discouraged thereby from bringing children into the world or hindered in rearing them. As an argument against ameliorative legislation the diminished fertility of the better stocks is an entire *ignoratio elenchi*.

But even if the inferior stocks are breeding more rapidly than the better ones, we have still to ask whether the effect on the race is as serious as it seems. Observe I speak here of the race. I am not thinking of the social structure, but of the average of congenital endowment in the race, and I am asking how far this will be affected by the greater fertility of inferior stocks. To the older biological theory the question answered itself. The race progressed by the constant cutting off of the tail, and the consequent shifting forward of the mean point of capacity. The newer discoveries of Bateson and De Vries have shown that the problem is not so simple. It becomes more and more probable that racial progress depends not on the summation of small fluctuations that are constantly arising and dying away again, but on more definite mutations which, once arising, give birth to a new stock with a new mean point of its own. The individual descendants of the new stock will exhibit qualities which fluctuate about the new mean, but which tend always to return to it. The fluctuations, even if they persist for a generation or two, are not permanently transmitted. They arise and die away again. The mutations, on the other hand, are of permanent significance. Now any large fluctuation may have the same outward appearance as a true mutation, but its effect as seen in subsequent generations will be quite different. There is in considerations of heredity no adequate ground for eliminating the one, and every ground for eliminating the other; and to apply biological conceptions scientifically in practice we ought to be able to make sure to which class any particular stock evincing some bad quality is to be referred. Now it is not probable that a large population like that of a modern nation is all of one fundamental type, and that all the individual differences are mere fluctuations. But it is probable that the many fundamental strains that constitute it are intricately blended, and that the variations of individuals arise partly from the conditions of breeding and partly from fluctuations of germinal quality. If this is so, it may well be that the same fundamental strains are permeating the whole of society and are perpetuated without alteration, although one part of society may be more fertile than another. Furthermore, many peculiarities of quality are traceable to laws of blending. A black and a splashed-white Andalusian fowl when mated give rise to a blue, but the black and white germinal elements are permanent, and reappear in known proportions in subsequent generations. Now there is much in what we know of psychological conditions to suggest that the laws of blending may be of even greater importance in psychological than in physical genetics. For we rarely find that individuals differ by the distinct presence or absence of some specific quality. On analysis mental or moral differences are apt to resolve themselves into differences in proportion and in the combination of elements. It is quite possible then that two strains, each sound in itself, should when united produce a bad result, and it may turn out that the true problem of eugenics is not one of selective breeding but of selective mating. Stocks *a* and *b* which when mated give rise to idiots or deaf-mutes, may quite conceivably mate with stocks *c* and *d* to engender normal children. I do not say that this is so. I suggest only that it is one of the possibilities to be taken into account. And there is a further point. It may be that some stocks undesirable in themselves contain strains that suitably blended with others are of value to the rational character as a whole. It may be that a roving and undisciplined disposition, which so often makes a vagrant, sometimes carries the strain from which originality and even genius arise. It may be that some of the milder and gentler strains give rise to weaklings, but yet are necessary in the general constitution of the stock to temper the harder material. We might easily disturb the balance of the stock on a whole by practising unwarily upon some of its component parts. At least such possibilities indicate the mass of work that has to be done in the field of heredity before we can safely apply its conceptions to the practical work of advancing social progress.

But, however this may be, I would emphasize this distinction in the biological outlook. The older Galtonian view working with small variations leads to the suggestion that natural selection is a permanent necessity of racial progress; it desires to subordinate the social structure in general to that end, and would, if consistently pushed through, lead to the permanent suppression, generation after generation, of the weaker stocks. The newer view points in quite another direction. It finds the basis of racial progress in definite mutations, which, if not destroyed by an unfavorable environment, establish themselves, and are not impaired by the preservation of individual descendants which manifest the new quality less perfectly than others. On this view it may be said that the most fundamental necessity from the point of view of racial progress is to maintain an environment in which any new mutation of promise socially considered may thrive and grow, and by this line of argument we arrive once more at the conclusion that liberty, equality of opportunity, and the social atmosphere of justice and considerateness are the most eugenic of agencies. On the other hand, there may in this view exist not only bad fluctuations, but some bad strains, and if these can be isolated out and definitely ascertained, to eliminate them would be work that, if it is to be done at all, would have to be done once and would not need to be done again. The general problem of eugenics, then, would be to produce an environment of welcome to socially useful mutations; its specific task to determine whether certain strains of bad tendency could be isolated out, and, if so, to consider whether their perpetuation could be arrested by means compatible with civilized ethics. On these lines eugenic ideas will, I can quite believe, be found to have a function in the work of social regeneration, though their application must for the most part await the progress of biological knowledge. On the other hand, there is no shadow of justification for the wild words in which eugenic writers frequently condemn the whole trend of what they call social legislation. I find, for example, in an early number of the *Eugenics Review* prominence given to a letter to the *Times* of May 26, 1909, from which I take the following passages:—

"Not only does Parliament in its so-called wisdom fail to apply science to the production of hereditary legislators, but in all recent social legislation it has actually penalized the fitter classes of society in the interests of the less fit. . . . The least fit class in the country is the old people who have failed to provide any savings against their old age, and that large class of cheats who manage to pretend that they are in that case. Such so-called social legislation tends to act in the same way. The birth-rate of the fitter is diminishing year by year, and we calmly sit by and watch the consequent degeneration of our race with idle hands. We take the human rubbish that emerges and give it compulsory education, Housing Acts, inspection of all sorts and at all seasons, at the expense of the fitter class, and imagine that better results will ensue than if we left the whole business alone. Are we right? or are the horse breeders right? They have demonstrably improved the race horses and with great rapidity. The old system of "let alone" also improved, though more slowly, the race of men. It is only the modern system of penalizing the fit for the sake of the unfit that seems to be put in action simultaneously with, if it does not cause, an observed race degeneration." [1]

This might pass as an individual opinion, but it is adopted very cordially by the *Eugenics Review*, the recognized and authoritative exponent of the eugenics movement in England.

"The views he expresses coinciding, as they do, so remarkably with our own, are those of an outsider who has wandered far and wide keeping his eyes open. Like Monsieur Jourdain with his prose, he talks our eugenic language without knowing it. This is why we gladly reproduce in full what he has so well said."

A recent number of the *Review* [2] is wholly dedicated to the criticism of the Poor Law Reports from the eugenic point of view, and though this is upon the whole far more discriminating, and the crudities above quoted are by implication rejected as the ignorant prejudices of

[1] *Eugenics Review*, July, 1909, pp. 66, 67.   [2] November, 1910.

outsiders, yet the line of criticism taken illustrates, to say the least, a tendency which has to be very carefully watched. Both branches of the commission, we are told (p. 172), started with the assumption that the pauper was a normal person made necessitous by circumstances. Such round generalization will surprise any one who has carefully studied the two reports. The majority report, in particular, is the work of persons who are well known to have carried their emphasis on character almost to what seemed to some of their critics to be the breaking point; and, broadly speaking, having studied the two reports with care, I may say roundly that in both, though in different ways, the aim is precisely not to overlook individual character, but to achieve a just demarcation of the legitimate spheres of social and individual responsibility. Take, for example, the treatment of unemployment. It is perfectly true that some of those who are in this condition suffer from defect of their own, whether congenital or acquired, but no one looking at the question as a whole, no one even acquainted with the elementary figures published month by month in the English *Labor Gazette*, can overlook the part played by social changes for which the individual is not responsible. Now, what is the recommendation of the commissioners? In both cases alike, though with differences of detail, the object is to save from hardship the man who is suffering from social changes which he cannot control, and thereby to make it possible for the first time to deal, with due disciplinary rigor, with him whose idleness is voluntary, and to apply curative and reformatory measures to those whose misfortunes are due to incapacity. The thesis of the minority report, in particular, is that the wastrel cannot be dealt with satisfactorily until he is parted, by a clear line of demarcation, from the man whose troubles are due to circumstance, and from the eugenic point of view what better beginning could be made? If we are to discover whether wastrels are men of degenerate stock, and if we are ultimately to take measures to prevent the degenerate stock from breeding, there is one preliminary condition that we must realize ; we must first know that the stocks that we are dealing with are in reality hopeless, and for this purpose we must first have our social conditions so adjusted that all men who are in reality capable of adapting themselves to a well-ordered social organization shall have the opportunity of proving what is in them. The social environment must be established upon ethical lines before we can say that the successful are the fit, or that the unsuccessful deserve elimination.

In support of its opinion that pauperism is in the main a hereditary taint, the *Eugenics Review* proceeds in all solemnity to narrate the lamentable history of a number of pauper families, as though hereditary pauperism were a new phenomenon or one of which Poor Law administrators had not long since learned to take account. We know there are hereditary paupers, but to begin with we have to ask what is the nature of the heredity, and I find no attempt to make this discrimination in the pages of the *Review*.[1] A is a pauper, and his children, B, C, and D, are paupers, and D marries another pauper, and

---

[1] See p. 187, where the fact that successive generations of the same family contains an undue proportion of paupers is made to point to the conclusion that pauperism is due to inherent defects which are hereditarily transmitted !

of their children again three out of four are paupers. No doubt. But the Eugenist seems to forget that all classes are in the main hereditary. The average individual is he who neither rises much above nor sinks below the position in which he is born; and as an individual of average endowments born in the landlord or the professional or the artisan class will become a landlord, professional man, or an artisan; so the individual of average endowments born in pauperism may be expected to remain in the confines of pauperism. If we would know generally how much of the heritage of pauperism is due to the conditions under which the children make their start in life, and how much to hereditary taint, there is one method of determination. It is that of securing equal opportunity to the least and to the most fortunate, and to secure this equal opportunity is a problem of reorganizing institutions. Against any such reorganization, proceeding open-eyed with a clear view of individual differences, the eugenic criticism is wholly beside the mark.

The whole of the argument admits of being summed up in a few sentences. So far as the eugenic principle advocates the substitution of rational for natural selection, it is, in the abstract, upon firm ground. Where it can be clearly established that a stock is tainted with a hereditary blemish so great as to outweigh its merits, it is desirable that that stock should not be perpetuated. That is already recognized ethically as a duty and is acted on by many individuals, in cases where there is such a taint as that of insanity. There is every reason why our knowledge on these matters should be carried further and systematized, and it is possible that in certain cases it may be found desirable to crystallize ethical sentiment in positive law; for example, in the case of such a class as the feeble-minded, where permanent care is desirable for the benefit of the individual, it may be right that, as a condition of such care, restriction from marriage should be insisted on by society in the future interest of the race. On the other hand, the use of eugenic arguments against legislation designed to replace the struggle for existence by ordered social cooperation is at bottom a misapplication of the principle. It rests on the survival of the older ideas of natural selection under a new form, in new terminology. The method of social legislation should not be to accommodate institutions to the survival of the stronger; it should be to bring the social structure into accordance with sound principles of social coöperation. In such a system those who are fit in the true sense of the term, those, that is to say, who are capable of becoming useful members of the social organization, can find their place; and it is only when all such persons are endowed with full opportunities to adapt themselves to social requirements that the failures of society can be legitimately regarded as the unfit. Those who so prove their unfitness are then legitimate objects for institutional tutelage, and it will then for the first time become possible to enter into the question of their right to propagate their like. That question would then be determined by the light that our knowledge of heredity could throw upon the future of their descendants. These views do not appear to me to be out of accord with the sounder teaching of the more cautious biologists. They conflict only with those enthusiasts who make rash applications based on confusion of the new teaching with the old. To illustrate this contrast I cannot do better than set side by side the sociological applications which Professor Bateson would make of Mendelian principles with the deductions drawn from his remarks by an enthusiastic reviewer in the pages of the *Eugenics Review*. Let us hear first the reviewer, Mr. G. P. Mudge, in the *Eugenics Review* for July, 1909, p. 137 : —

"With regard to man, it is now clear that what social reform, legislation, and philanthropy have failed to accomplish, can be achieved by biology. Tell the student of genetics what type of nation we desire, within the limits of the characters which the nation already possesses, and confer upon him adequate powers, and he will evolve it. It is not too much to say that, if he were instructed to evolve a "fit" nation, *i.e.* one of self-reliant and self-supporting individuals, in the course of a few generations there would be neither workhouses, hospitals, unemployables, congenital criminals, or drunkards.

"Students of eugenics will turn with interest to the concluding pages of Professor Bateson's book; there he deals with the sociological application of the science of genetics. We commend every advocate of social panaceas and of legislative interference with natural processes to read this part of the book. In a few well-chosen sentences he gives expression to the judgment of every biologist, alike of the present and the past, who has given to social problems adequate and unbiassed thought. For nothing is more evident to the naturalist than that we cannot convert inherent vice into innate virtue, nor change "leaden instincts into golden conduct," nor "transform a sow's ear into a silken purse" by any known social process. Our vast and costly schemes of free, compulsory, elementary education, of County Council scholarships and evening classes, which are among these social processes supposed to possess the magic virtue of transforming the world into a fairyland, may be a delusion and a danger. And so, too, may be all the other well-intentioned but costly panaceas that harass and tax and eventually destroy the fit in order to attempt, for they can never achieve, the salvation of the unfit."

Let us turn from these sweeping condemnations, these triumphant prophecies, these large assertions of the powers of the biologist, to Professor Bateson's own words, the very words to which we are referred in justification of Mr. Mudge's statement. They are, unfortunately, too long to quote as a whole, but I will take the leading points.

"To the naturalist it is evident that, while the elimination of the hopelessly unfit is a reasonable and prudent policy for society to adopt, any attempt to distinguish certain strains as superior and to give special encouragement to them would probably fail to accomplish the object proposed and most certainly be unsafe."

Contrast this with the proclamation, "Tell the student of genetics what type of nation we require . . . he will evolve it." Let us turn back again to Professor Bateson: —

"Some serious physical and mental defects, almost certainly also some morbid diatheses and some of the forms of vice and criminality, could be eradicated if society so determined. That, however, is the utmost length to which the authority of physiological science can, in the present state of knowledge, be claimed for interference. More extensive schemes are already being advocated by writers who are neither utopians nor visionaries. Their proposals are directed in the belief that society is more likely to accept a positive plan for the encouragement of the fit than negative interference for the restraint of the unfit. Genetic science, as I have said, gives no clear sanction to these proposals. It may also be doubted whether the guiding estimate of popular sentiment is well founded. Society has never shown itself averse to adopt measures of the most stringent and even brutal kind for the control of those whom it regards as its enemies.

"Genetic knowledge must certainly lead to new conceptions of justice, and it is by no means impossible that, in the light of such knowledge, public opinion will welcome measures likely to do more for the extinction of the criminal and degenerate than has been accomplished by ages of penal enactment."

With so cautious and reasoned a statement social philosophy can in principle have no ground of quarrel. It can only desire that the data may be as fully as possible ascertained and, in proportion as civic effort succeeds in reorganizing the social structure on the basis of justice and equity, it will be prepared to deal with the strains, if they exist, with which a life in accordance with equity is incompatible.

CHAPTER IV

Social Harmony and the Social Mind

Our conclusions so far are two. First, the biological conditions of human development are not such as to present any insuperable barrier to progress. Second, we may expect to find progress, if anywhere, rather in social than in racial modifications. But before we inquire further whether progress is a fact to be discovered in this direction, we must consider more carefully what progress is. Hitherto we have been content with describing it as a process of the realization of ends of human value, ethical ends. We must seek to define this conception, not indeed with the fullness which it deserves, but sufficiently for our purpose, that is, for the purpose of estimating the trend of evolution. We must form a closer definition of progress, and then compare it with the actual course of evolution, if we are to obtain a plain answer to the question whether the movement of social evolution in general or the evolution of any given society in particular is or has been a movement of progress.

There is a tendency, calling itself scientific, to dispense with one side of this question and to educe the conception of value from the trend of evolution itself. I need hardly before this audience spend time in combating this confusion or argue at length that history is not philosophy. In describing the process by which things have come to be what they are, we are not justifying their existence. We may incidentally bring to light facts which serve for their justification, or possibly for their excuse, if to understand all is to pardon all. But this is not of the essence of the matter. Rational justification and historical narrative belong to two different orders of investigation. Nor, again, if we prove the existence of a tendency, do we thereby prove that that tendency is desirable. Few would affirm the contrary in black and white. Yet if we look at the kind of argument that is popular in the press or on the platform, we must admit that very many people slide with the greatest apparent ease from the one point of view to the other. To show that a certain line of policy accords with the tendencies of the day, that it is a part of our manifest destiny as a nation, that it is inevitable, and so forth, are highly popular rhetorical devices for recommending it to the desires, and even to the consciences of mankind. As a social creature man does not like to be left out in the cold. He loves to be in the swim, and when he is told that his side is winning, that its success is so certain that his own vote is little more than a formality, he makes all the more haste to record that vote, and add his unit to the swelling majority. In this way and by such means as these do prophecies become the causes of their own fulfilment. It requires some detachment, not indeed to admit in the abstract, but to hold fast in the concrete the simple truth that of existing tendencies some may be good, some bad, and some indifferent, and that it is the function of a reasoning creature to choose among them and throw in his weight with the best.

There is indeed one theory on which a rational choice

becomes impossible. If society moves by a mechanical necessity in which the will of human beings plays no part, there is no need to discuss what is desirable or the reverse. The only question of interest is what will be, and whether it ought to be is an academic point of no practical concern. Whether this theory is tenable is a question on which our discussion as it advances will, I hope, throw some light. But I may for the sake of clearness say this much in advance. We shall have to recognize not merely the existence, but the constant extension of mind, of will, and therefore of human choice as an actual force in the evolution of society, and if we are right in this, it follows that the general belief that some tendency is desirable is a factor to be seriously taken into account in estimating its future. This conclusion is not necessarily inconsistent with a certain form of rational determinism, but it is inconsistent with any mechanical or materialist theory which renders rational conceptions of value practically insignificant. But if we reject any such theory, and admit the influence of rational choice on social tendencies, there is good reason for a systematic inquiry which shall enable us to decide what tendencies are upon the whole desirable or otherwise.

In thus admitting the necessity of a social philosophy I am aware that I have given hostages to fortune. You may reasonably call upon me to stand and deliver the said philosophy, and unless I am prepared to do so, you may decline to listen to anything further that I have to say on social progress. But on my side I may be allowed to put in a plea of mitigation, and it is one which I am sure will appeal to you. A complete exposition of a social philosophy would involve a searching inquiry into the first principles of value, that is to say into ethics, and even, I fear, into metaphysics as well. You would not thank me if, at this stage and with the amount of time at our disposal, I were to call on you to follow me into an inquiry of this magnitude. But if I dispense you from the labor of listening to such a disquisition, you on your part must allow me to make certain initial assumptions. I will be as modest as possible. I will not assume that life is something intrinsically good, but I must assume that the good for man is to be found in some kind of life, not in the negation of life. I will not assume that fullness of vitality is as such desirable, but I must assume that, other things equal, the fuller life is on the whole the more desirable. I will not assume that happiness, however attained, is good, but I must assume that there is some form of happiness which is good, or, at lowest, that misery is an evil. I will not assume that the full realization of the capacities of mind defines the end of life, but I must assume that some form of such realization is an integral element in a desirable life. Finally, I will not assume that all social life is good, still less that social growth is necessarily a change for the better, but I must assume that a life which is completely social — which fully realizes the social capacities of man — is good, and that if we use the phrase "social development" in a precise sense as a short expression for the accomplishment of such a life, social development is good. All these assumptions can, of course, be made the subject of philosophic criticism. It is held by many that the good for man, or the least evil, consists really in negation, not in greater fullness of life, but in the restriction of effort and the eventual overcoming of the will to live. It is held by many that the good is not to be sought in this life at all, but in preparation for another. It is held that the general all-round development of mind is a secondary matter, that the beginning of true wisdom is just the submission of the soul to the Guiding Will. It is held that social life is of secondary moment, and that what matters for each man is to discipline his own heart and to save his own soul. Thus I am aware that in setting out my position I am making assumptions, and I do not claim for these assumptions the character of axiomatic truths. On the contrary, I think them capable of proof, and on another occasion I should be willing to submit them to the test. For the present I set them up merely as assumptions, to show you the basis on which I am proceeding, and the only test to which I shall subject them is the indirect one of drawing out some of their results and showing you whither they lead us.

I may begin with the conception of social development, and I will endeavor to define it a little further and to see how it stands related to our other assumptions. Now the full meaning of a term like development is to be approached rather through concrete experience than by the road of abstract definition. Yet here and there an abstract definition may help us, and no help is to be despised. As to this particular term, I shall not attempt any new definition. I shall content myself for the present with the familiar conception of maturation of that which previously existed in germ, the active realization of something which is at first a mere potentiality. These are terms which in the end will require a far closer examination, but that examination I must ask you on this occasion to forego. I remind you only that in general the process of development involves quantitative growth and increase, so that, for example, if we speak of the development of mind, we mean that there is more mind, that it becomes a larger factor in life, that it covers a wider sphere. To this it must be added that all organic growth involves a correlated series of changes among parts that operate in concert. It is never mere quantitative extension. It is a process by which many elements emerge into definite characteristic distinctness, while maintaining unimpaired unity. So much it is well to bear in mind as to development in general. But as to social development a little more must be said: —

(1) Society exists in individuals. When all the generations through which its unity subsists are counted in, its life is their life, and nothing outside their life. The individuals themselves, indeed, are profoundly modified by the fact that they form a society, for it is through the social relation that they realize the greater part of their own achievements. Each man is, so to say, the meeting point of a great number of social relations. Each such relation depends on him, on his qualities, on his actions, and also affects him and modifies his qualities and his actions. The whole complex of such relations constitutes the life of society. It follows that social development is also in the end personal or individual development. If society develops in any given direction, the persons constituting it develop accordingly, and if development as such means a movement towards a fuller and more complete life, then social development means a movement towards a fuller and more complete life for the persons of whom society consists.

It will not escape your notice that this conclusion makes a tacit postulate of no small moment. It postulates a possible harmony between the claims of different persons, and that such a harmony can be found is, I think, the fundamental postulate of social ethics. It is not an unproven or unprovable postulate. On the contrary, I think that proof of it can be adduced. But to offer that proof would take me into the region of ethical first principles, into which, as I have said, I can hardly ask you now to follow me. In default you must let me assume such a harmony to be possible; and to find the way and means thereto then becomes the problem of social ethics. It was the mistake of some earlier writers, especially of a certain school of economists, to assume that the lines of harmony were so clearly prescribed by the very nature of mankind that each man had only to follow his own apparent interest, and the best possible social results would ensue. Life unfortunately is not so simple. The operation of enlightened self-interest leading each man along the path of least resistance to the goal of greatest desire does not produce social peace or social progress. The line of harmony is rather the narrow path, every divergence from which involves collision and more or less of frustration and misery to some one. It is not any and every development of the individual which is socially desirable, or even socially possible. For if one man's personality gains till he bestrides the narrow world like a Colossus, then it remains for the rest to peep in and out and find themselves dishonored graves. His overgrown development means for the mass not development, but extinction; and in lesser degree a similar discord results from every development of the individual which is not in accordance with the conditions of social harmony. Social development, then, involves the harmonious development of the constituent members of society. This is one of the elements of truth contained in what is called the organic conception of society. To speak of society as if it were a physical organism is a piece of mysticism, if indeed it is not quite meaningless. But the life of society and the life of an individual do resemble one another in certain respects, and the term "organic" is as justly applicable to the one as to the other. For an organism is a whole consisting of interdependent parts. Each part lives and functions and grows by subserving the life of the whole. It sustains the rest and is sustained by them, and through their mutual support comes a common development. And this is how we would conceive the life of man in society in so far as it is harmonious.[1]

[1] This explanation may serve to meet an objection which may have occurred to you when I laid down that social development implied the development of the persons constituting society. You might ask, does the phrase "persons" mean all of those constituting the given society, or some only? May it not be shown that there are developments, *e.g.* the rise of aristocracy, which involve a development of one class and one kind of social activity, but a suppression of others? The reply is that such developments are only partial, that they imply arrest, that what there is of social progress in them does involve a development of individuals, while, on the other hand, in so far as the life of any member of society is cramped and mutilated by them, there is social stagnation and decay. Any such development is not fully harmonious. Gain on one side is set off by loss on another. The problem of true social progress is to find the lines on which development on one side does not retard development on another, but assists it.

Two other possible misunderstandings may be noted here. The term "social development" might be used to cover mere quantitative growth in territory or population, which would not imply personal

(2) Society, and particularly civilized society, is a very complex structure. We have not to do with one society, — the political community standing over against a number of individuals who are its component members. Each individual is a member of many societies. He is one of a family; he belongs to a church, to a corporation, to a trade union, to a political party. He is also a citizen of his state, and his state has a place in the commonwealth of states. In so far as the world becomes one, that is to say, as social relations arise which interconnect human beings all the world over, Humanity becomes the supreme society, and all smaller social groupings may be conceived as constituent elements of this supreme whole. Now what has been said of individuals applies *mutatis mutandis* to every social group. Such a group, for example the family, realizes some of the characteristic qualities and capacities of human beings, occupies a certain share of their affections, their energies, their intelligence. Every such group accordingly has its claim to share in social development, just as the individual has his claim. Its development, so far as it can be harmonized with the other claims of social life, is for the good. Accordingly, the problem of the social order is not to realize the kind of abstract unity which has sometimes been put forward by the makers of Utopias from Plato downwards. The

development. But that is not the sense in which the phrase is here used. Secondly, social development is crystallized in institutions, and even in material capital; and it might be suggested that such growth does not imply corresponding enlargement of the individual life. It may be replied that so far as this is true there is misdirection of energy, and the social achievement of the past is not making for social development in the present.

ideal development of society is not the fashioning of a self-contained political state which should supersede the necessity for all the spontaneous associations of human beings which fill so large a part of actual life. It consists rather in the discovery of the lines upon which these manifold forms of human association can be brought each to its fullest pitch of efficiency as a part of a wider organization. Thus that form of family organization is the best which gives the most complete expression to the love of husband and wife, parent and child, without cramping the development of personality on the one side or impeding the development of collective responsibility on the other. I may best illustrate what I mean by referring to certain arguments based on a quite legitimate regard for the institution of the family with which we are familiar in the controversies of the day. Thus, on the one hand, measures for securing equitable treatment of the wife and child have been, if they are no longer, resisted on the ground that they undermine the authority of the husband and father, and therewith the solidity of the family life. This was to push the ideal of the family unity without regard to the claims of personality. On the other hand, public education and public care for children generally have been, and still are, frequently criticized on the ground that they are undermining parental responsibility. This again is to push the ideal of the family to the prejudice of a legitimate development of a wider public responsibility. The method which our principle suggests is that the precise limits of the sphere of parental responsibility are to be determined by our experience of the results. We by no means deny that responsibility. We regard it as a necessary consequence of an institution of the highest value to man. But if we find that it is actually failing in any given direction, as for example it failed in the matter of education, to perform a necessary social function, we must not ignore the claims of that function. We must look to other means of fulfilling it, and must accordingly draw the line between the responsibility of the parent and that of the state at a new point, so that as far as possible the claims of the parental tie, the claims of the child, and the claims of the public conscience may coöperate and not antagonize. I do not say that the point is easy to find, or that all problems are solved merely by being stated in this form. I say that they cannot be solved until they are conceived on these lines; that as long as any one duty, any one right, or generally the claims of any one social relation are regarded as absolute or are maintained without regard to the similar claims of other rights, other social relations, nothing but a lop-sided and in the end self-destructive form of social development is possible.

We can once again help ourselves with the organic metaphor without allowing it to dominate us. The developed organism contains minor organisms within it. The living body is made up of organs and the organs of cells, and the cell itself is a living organism. Now the life of the body is not perfected by suppressing the life of the cells, but by maintaining it at its highest point of efficiency. Nor is the organism developed by reducing the cells to a uniform type, but rather by allowing each type to vary on its own lines, provided always that the several variations are in the end mutually compatible. These things are applicable to society, from the widest to the narrowest form thereof. If there is ever to be a world state, and if such a state is to be reconciled to permanent progress, it is to be achieved not by the suppression of nationality, but by the development of national differentiation; not by the suppression of political freedom, but through the spontaneous movement of self-governing communities. Similarly, if the sphere of action of the state within its own borders is to expand as it is doing daily in my own country, it must be, and in fact it is, not by the suppression of other forms of social cooperation nor by the destruction of individual life, but in such wise and on such lines as upon the whole liberates activity and provides lines of harmonious development for the constituent parts. In a word, the conception of harmonious development applies not only to individuals, but to the various possible forms of human association.

At this stage it will appear that starting from one of our assumptions and seeking to define it we have been led to include our other assumptions along with it. We have conceived social development as a development of individuals in harmony. In so doing we have covered the conceptions (a) of a fuller vitality and (b) of the realization of mental or spiritual capacity, which were two of the remaining elements which we postulated as going to constitute the end or good of man. It will be remembered that we carefully refrained from assuming that any sort of individual development was good. We assumed only that the good must admit of some kind of development, and we are now able to say what kind. It is that kind in which all members of a society can share. It is such that its pursuit by one, far from hindering, positively promotes its pursuit by another. It is the kind of development, that is, which can be pursued by many in harmony. This does not mean that there is only one type of good citizen. The kind of development which is social is a very wide genus, admitting of numerous and highly contrasted specific differences, and, as we know, many of the most important functions of a man depend not on his likeness to others, but on his individuality. Conversely it is an important part of the development of social harmony that it comes to make use of wider and more complex divergencies of individuals. Of these we need not speak further for the moment. We remark only that the idea of social development covers that of individual development in the only sense in which this idea can be applied to a plurality of individuals whose lives affect one another. Lastly, with the development of the individual conceived as a center of social relations, the idea of happiness is, I imagine, involved. The full discussion of this question would take us far afield. I must leave it to you to consider whether either happiness or misery is to be found elsewhere in those things which make or mar the development of personality, in itself, in its relations to others, or in its capacity as a part which has a function to perform in a life infinitely greater than its own.

Our assumptions it will be seen tend to come down to one. In other words approaching the problem of the good or the desirable from several sides and roughly formulating several elements that appear to express a part of its meaning we find on analysis that these several conceptions lead up to a center. This central conception is the idea of a harmony in the manifold developments of life. Our assumption then is that the good lies in this direction, and progress will consist accordingly in the movement by which such harmony may be realized.

Now this principle of harmony has many applications which cannot be drawn out here. There is a harmony within the life of the individual, and a harmony of man with his physical environment as well as the harmony of man in society. All these are parts of a whole, and all are elements in the life that may be called good or desirable. But in all its meanings harmony, as already hinted, is something which does not come of itself, but is achieved in greater or less degree by effort, that is to say, by intelligence and will. Hence the conditions of harmony rest on the nature of mind, and to understand the growth of harmony we must follow up the growth of mind. The study of this growth belongs in a sense to psychology, but it must not be forgotten that the highest forms of mental activity, from the most elementary general ideas upward, are not merely individual, but social products.

All higher psychology is in a sense social psychology. Thus our ideas from a very early stage clothe themselves in language, and language is a social product. Now our ideas may be suggested in the first instance by personal experience, and I do not deny that they may precede and do continually outstrip the means of expression. None the less, the form which they take is largely determined by the means of expression which enable us to fix, utilize, and build with one while another remains a vague suggestion, of which perhaps we finally lose hold. It is the common experience wherein we find the thoughts of others responding to our own that most readily acquires substantive shape and form. Moreover, the greater part of each man's personal experience is made up out of his interaction with others in the multifarious relations of life, and these relations, from the earliest known phases of human society, are controlled by customs which arise out of the needs of social life and are maintained by the social tradition. Through this tradition society exerts a continuous control over the individual, of which avowed and obvious coercion is the least important element. The vital factor is that from infancy upwards the social milieu into which he is born interpenetrates his thought and will, and turns his individuality into a creation of the time and place of his life. Even the strongest individualities do not, strictly speaking, resist this process. They react to it more powerfully than others, so as to produce some marked divergence from the ordinary type. Very often the divergence consists in this, that the strong individual is just the typical man of his time carried to a higher power. Otherwise he may be in various degrees original, peculiar, perhaps eccentric, but even in his eccentricity he will still exhibit the joint resultant of social and individual forces.

It is thus easy to understand that though there is no thought except in the mind of an individual thinker, yet the thought of any generation, and indeed of each individual in the generation, is a social product. But we must go further than this. The sum of thought in existence at any time is something more than any thought that exists in the head of any individual; it is something to which many minds contribute, and which yet may be for many purposes a real unity. Consider an advanced complex science. No one thinks the whole of such a science at any moment. Perhaps no one lives who is master of it all. Yet the whole range of truth that the science has elaborated is available for social or individual uses. It is recorded in books. It is, so to say, incorporated in instruments and laboratories, whereby the results worked out by one man for one purpose are available by another man for another purpose. The science is more than the living knowledge of any individual. It is social knowledge or social thought, not in the sense that it exists in the mind of a mystical social unit, nor in the sense that it is the common property of all men, which it certainly is not, but in the sense that it is the product of many minds working in conscious or unconscious cooperation, that it forms a part of the permanent social tradition going constantly to shape the thought and direct the efforts of fresh generations of learners, — that, in a word, it has all the permanency and potency which the individual has not. We might easily apply the same reasoning to other departments of thought, to philosophy, to religion, to the literary and imaginative representation of life, and to the common sense knowledge that at once expresses and helps to form the experience of ordinary men in ordinary relations. The thought of any society at any time is a social thought. This social thought forms the point of departure for individuals who are brought up in it, perhaps go beyond it and contribute something fresh of their own, perhaps fail fully to assimilate and fall short of it.

As there is a social thought, so there is a social will. Again, that does not necessarily mean that there exist objects common to all or to the great majority of the members of any community. There may be such objects, — for example, the successful pursuit of a war in which the pride of a nation is involved, — and in that case the social will has a very easily intelligible meaning and a simple definable object. But the social will is more permanent and pervasive than this. It covers all those modes of action that the existing constitution of society dictates, all the institutions that it maintains, all the customs that it prescribes. Many of these, particularly in the lower forms of society, may never be thought out, may never be so much as examined or considered by any thinking individual in their bearing on the actual life of society. But to say this is merely to emphasize their social as opposed to their personal genesis. Customs may and do arise, for example, purely from the action of individuals, each seeking ends of his own, and as they are imitated and pass with the approval or at least without the disapproval of others, they rapidly crystallize and become recognized modes in which a man may and should comport himself under given circumstances. Thus the forces governing action are social, not necessarily in the sense that they are governed by a broad conception of social ends, but in the sense that they are the products of the social connection between man and man.

What has been said may suffice to show that when we speak of social thought, social will, or more generally of social mind, we neither imply a mystical psychic unity nor a fully achieved consciousness of the social life on the part of the component members of society. Such a consciousness is in fact a developed product of the social mind, but its presence is not to be assumed wherever the term "social mind" is used. This term is simply an expression for the mass of ideas operative in a society, communicable from man to man, and serving to direct the thoughts and actions of individuals. The kind of unity which attaches to the social mind is not definable in general terms. It varies from case to case. In the more complex societies there are for example many institutions, each with its distinct ethos, and the existence of this ethos means that the institution lays a plastic hand on all who enter it, and with greater or less thoroughness moulds their life and actions. As an individual may and probably does belong to more than one institution, he is subject to influences of this kind from more than one quarter. There is thus in a sense more than one social mind that claims him, and this alone will suffice to warn us against the supposition that the social mind is necessarily something common, for example, to all members of the same political community.[1] Such a community may indeed, if highly developed, possess a very clear unity of its own, and enjoy a very distinct order of ideas, marking out the behavior of its members in no uncertain fashion. But if highly developed it probably is the seat of many constituent institutions, each with a corresponding ethos, tradition, or mind of its own, operating on its own members in similar fashion. By the social mind, then, we mean not necessarily a unity pervading any given society as a whole, but a tissue of

[1] It is for this reason that I prefer the term "social" to the term "general." The "general will" is an entity not always to be discovered, and the use of the term leads to the most inhuman torture of evidence to prove that there is a generality of will where there is none.

operative psychological forces which in their higher developments crystallize into unity within unity, and into organism operating upon organism. We mean something essentially of psychological character that arises from the operations of masses of men, and molds and is in turn remolded by the operation of masses of men; which has no existence except in the minds of men, and yet is never fully realized in the mind of any one man; which depends on the social relations between man and man, but takes full cognizance of the relation only in the higher stages of its development.

As the function of the individual mind is to organize the life of the individual, so the function of the social mind is to organize the life of society, to control the physical environment, and to regulate the relations of members of the community to one another and of the community as a whole to other communities. This function is of course more adequately performed in proportion as the social mind develops. Now the development of mind in general consists partly in increase of width or scope. The developed mind has a wider reach. Its grasp extends further over the future and the past. Its insight into reality probes deeper, and in consequence its practical control of life is greater. Secondly, the development of mind lies in increased clearness, articulateness, connectedness of perception and of thought. It takes a more penetrating and concrete, and at the same time a more rational and connected view. Lastly, and this has special application to the social mind, the more developed mind is more completely and consciously a unity. In the case of the individual, indeed, a unity may always be predicated by another person, even if it be not conscious. An animal or a child may, for all we know, have no thought of yesterday or tomorrow, but we onlookers are aware that it is one and the same being throughout. In the case of the social mind, on the other hand, the consciousness of unity profoundly affects the unity itself. One is tempted to say that it actually brings it to birth. This, however, would not be true in all cases, for the minds of men who are brought into contact affect one another, and may give to any society a certain oneness, marking it out from others, without perhaps any consciousness of the relation. Moreover, when a new and wider unity is recognized, it is recognized as something already existing, as a relation which was present and was operative somehow while yet unknown. But however this be, any developed unity in the social mind rests on a consciousness, first of some special relation of each individual constituting it to his fellow members, and secondly of the group, society, institution itself as a whole. In its more concrete developments then the social mind has a certain measure of conscious unity as its basis, and both the solidity and the extent of this conscious unity are of importance in determining its power; solidity because this determines the effectiveness of social cooperation within its limits; extent because this determines the limits themselves. A rude society, a clan of warlike mountaineers, for instance, may be a very well-knit unity, conscious and proud of its clan life, but making little progress because it is at war with all its neighbors. An aggregation of such clans presents no unity, but only a scene of anarchy. Supposing them reduced to order by the strong hand of some *pax*

Romana or *pax Britannica*, there will be both loss and gain — gain in the widening of the social unit, loss in the vigor of social life. There will be some elements of a social relation over the whole aggregation, but it will be at least in the beginning a less lively union, an external order rather than the old hearty cooperation. Such compensating movements of gain and loss run right through the history of social development.

Now if we were to go at all closely into the nature of the unities which the social mind builds up, if in particular we should inquire how they are to be reconciled with the independent existence of the individual mind, and how one unity can overlap another, we should find ourselves repeating in essentials what has already been said of the conception of harmony. We should find that the development of the individual conditions and is conditioned by every social group to which he belongs, and we should find that of the groups in turn the same thing holds. The many groups are necessarily related, and their relations, though giving rise at first sight to divergent impulses, need not lead to conflict. They may be subordinate to a higher unity, and this in fact is the line of progress. Thus the development of the social mind is the development of social harmony expressed in psychological terms. But the psychological conception takes us further. It covers not only the harmonious development, which is the end, but the control of conditions, which is the means to that end. Harmonious development is not reached by instinct, nor does it proceed of itself. For stable and assured progress it requires all the powers of the human mind, and more powers than have yet been brought to bear. The harmony of life rests on the control of conditions by the social mind. This control is in part self-control — the control which by means of ethical conceptions the members of society exercise over themselves and one another — over social relations. It is in part the control of other things, such, for example, as the physical conditions of health. The one may be regarded as itself a part of the harmony which we take as the end, the other as a necessary condition or means to that end.

Thus the growth of the social mind is a more complete measure of progress than the conception of harmony itself. It takes us nearer to the essence of the forces at work, which are psychological, and it enables us to view not only results, but conditions, which are results in the making. We may therefore take the growth of social mind and its control over the conditions of life as the measure of progress, and we shall have to ask how far progress so conceived is realized in the history of humanity.

CHAPTER V

Social Morphology

WE have now arrived at a rough definition of the nature and general conditions of progress, and our next step is to compare it with the ascertained facts of social evolution itself. Conceiving social evolution as the growth, maintenance, or decay of a fabric of human achievement accomplishing itself through the medium of what we call cumulative tradition, we have to ask what the general tendency of these changes is, and whether they conform to our conception of progress. Is there any truth in the common optimistic saying that progress is the law of social life, or is there more to be said for the pessimistic view that in all the whirl of change there are many ups and downs, but no net gain as judged by those human values in terms of which genuine progress is to be defined? Or is there discernible among the devious movements of social evolution some one tendency which may be regarded as progressive, and is this tendency marked with sufficient emphasis and distinctness to justify the hope of success for further social effort? If so, have any new conditions come into play which render the prospect before such effort more hopeful or the reverse? Before we can answer these questions adequately, we must cast a glance at the methods which the study of social life has at its disposal, and the objects which it can reasonably expect to attain.

In ordinary phrase, its aim is supposed to be the discovery of the laws of social evolution. But this expression contains several ambiguities. The term "law," always a somewhat unfortunate metaphor in the philosophy of science, is perhaps nowhere so replete with pitfalls as in its application to sociology. Without seeking to exhaust its ambiguities, I must lay stress on one distinction. A "law" in science seems properly to imply a connection which is necessary and universal. It states the conditions from which certain consequences uniformly flow. It is, in a word, a generalization. So if there is any general law of evolution, it should be one which should tell us the conditions under which evolution occurs, and enable us to infer that when these conditions are given one phase of growth will be followed by another and another in a determinate order. It should help us to generalize or to predict. Now I do not wish to raise here the difficult question how far generalization and prediction are attainable in sociology. I would remark only that very often when a law of evolution is spoken of, particularly in sociology, it would seem that what is actually ascertained is something of a different order. It is not a question of generalization, but of descriptive synthesis. A series of changes is passed in review and considered as a whole. So considered it presents a certain character, exhibits a certain trend. This trend is formulated, and the formula is described as the law of the series. But the conditions of the process are not ascertained, nor is it proved that the same series of changes would, if at once begun somewhere else, recur in the same order. There is no basis of generalization or of prediction.

Now it is important to recognize that such description is a legitimate, and may be a very important and a very difficult, object of investigation. Only it is quite distinct from the generalization with which it is often loosely confounded. It has its application not only in sociology, but in the field of organic life. In biological science we may find an example in the life history of an animal or plant from the first germ of life to adult growth, and thence to decay and death. When we learn, for example, that a given animal at a certain stage has gills and a tail and lives under the water, while later on it sheds its tail and gills, develops lungs and four legs and hops about on the ground, we have a rough sketch of the development of the common frog, which the natural history of that species will fill in as fully as may be desired. This, as it stands, is the history of a process rather than the establishment of a law. It is true that this particular history can be generalized, — what is true of one animal being true of a whole species under normal circumstances, — but the method is equally applicable if only one individual process be in question. Thus we might describe, so far as the geological record allows us, the life history of a whole species considered as a single totality. We might remark its rare appearance at one epoch, its growth in subsequent times, and its gradual extinction, and we might perhaps find certain varieties of form accompanying this growth and decay. So again in human history we can sketch an outline of the rise and fall of an ancient state, and here again we are giving a descriptive account of the broad character of a certain evolution, of a process which has a certain unity of its own and which appears only in a single instance.

SOCIAL MORPHOLOGY

In none of these cases is it accurate to speak of a law of evolution as being the end and object of our inquiry. Our purpose is rather to grasp a certain development as a whole; to measure the distance traversed from the first phase to the last; to bring the facts together in a synthesis; to be able, if we may so put it, to say what the whole amounts to. Such a synthesis yields not the law of evolution in general, but rather the trend or orbit of some particular evolution. We may make the point clear by considering the method of determining an orbit in the most literal sense of that term. We wish to ascertain the path along which a body moves. We may begin empirically by determining a number of positions which the body occupies in succession. The curve which it describes may then be ascertained by joining up these points. The result is to coördinate the data and enable us to judge the direction and extent of the movement. But so far the term "law" is inappropriate, since no universal and necessary relation of terms has been ascertained. We cannot be sure that the body will continue, beyond the points observed, to move in the same curve. What we have is just an accurate record of the magnitude and direction of the course which it has actually taken. But the motion of a body may also be determined in another way. It may be deduced from certain conditions to which it is known to be subject. Its curve will then be determined, as the mathematician will tell us, by a certain relation expressible in an equation between an ordinate and an abscissa, two governing conditions applying to every successive point along the length of the curve and by the fixed proportion between them governing its shape. The equation which expresses this proportion, then, is, in strictness, the law of the curve, and knowing this equation we can predict the movement of the body and the position which it will occupy at any moment. The curve as determined by the first method is a descriptive synthesis; as determined by the second, it is a true law. I need hardly add that in the order of discovery the first method may lead up to the second, the synthesis of empirical data preparing the way for analysis of underlying conditions. The first of these cases corresponds in our inquiry to the synthesis which enables us to formulate the historic movement of society; the second to the generalization which should assign the forces determining this movement, and therefore enable us to predict the future or infer the character of the unrecorded past. And it is again possible that from one result we might proceed to the other. For if we could resolve the life history of a frog or of an organic species, or the history of a state or of a civilization, into certain permanent factors correlated permanently in a definite manner, and could show that the result of this correlation was to produce the process which we find, we should then have not only the actual development as an historical fact, but a law of development. And it is the law of evolution in this sense, a general law, that is to say, dominating the whole evolutionary process, which constitutes the strict meaning of the term. To discover such a law or laws, we should have not only to know where the evolutionary process begins and in what it ends, but we should have to ascertain the factors underlying it throughout and by their interaction producing the concrete result.

The distinction may be illustrated once again from the theory of biological evolution. When Mr. Herbert Spencer conceives of evolution as a process at once towards higher integration and greater differentiation, he is giving a descriptive formula applicable to the evolutionary process as a whole. When, in relation to the organic world, Darwin arrives at the conception of the struggle for existence, the laws of heredity and natural selection, as causes determining the growth of species, he is giving us a theory of the permanent conditions underlying this development. Mr. Spencer's formula is descriptive; Darwin's is causational. Both formulæ have their value. To describe the whole in the sense of forming a synthesis in which all its parts should be seen in their various places would be a worthy object of scientific investigation, even if we should fail to ascertain the conditions upon which development depends, while to discover these conditions would be a further step.

Thus there are two distinct objects which the student of social evolution may set before himself. First of all he may endeavor to grasp the broad trend of social evolution; that is to say, he may attempt a synthesis of its successive phases, and here he might conceivably take the evolution of a single society, or of a type of civilization, or finally, of the whole of humanity for his subject. Provided that the process be grasped as a connected whole and that any illuminating description can be given of its trend and tendency, provided that he can find in it, as it were, any clear hint of definiteness of direction, the object will be a perfectly legitimate one for scientific endeavor. Secondly, he may seek to do what Darwin did with biology, and to discover not only the actual movement of society, but the permanent conditions upon which such movement depends. The first inquiry may, of course, throw light on the second. From our knowledge of the path on which evolution has moved we may naturally hope to obtain light on the forces which have moved it. But this, we shall find, will raise further and more difficult questions, and the first object in comparative sociology must be to effect the synthesis which will give us not the law but the path or trend. Even this we shall find to be a problem of great complexity and only to be approached by severely limiting the scope of inquiry.

It may be asked in what respect a descriptive formula of social evolution would differ from a sufficiently comprehensive social history. Suppose that we could take all sides of a nation's life, its politics and religion, its literature and art, its science and philosophy, its industry and commerce, and write their history in full, should we not have a final account of the actual facts of its social evolution, and would anything remain but to pass at once if we could to the causes connecting the different phases of the process? Would any formula of synthesis be necessary as an intermediate step? Well, in the first place it will readily be seen that the attempt to grasp this many-sided development as a whole, as forming one social evolution, carries us outside the conception of history as a narrative. We find ourselves at once dealing not with one history but with many. The history of science is one thing, that of literature another, and in a time like ours either of these is so rich and diversified in material that it would naturally break up into many component parts, each of which as a narrative would be separately pursued. Now if these different strands are somehow to be woven together so that we may form some conception of the rope which they constitute, quite another kind of intellectual effort is needed. We shall have to find, as it were, some common denominator for our different results. We shall have to analyze our data, to find the points at which the different lines of development impinge on one another, and so discover in the end how far they form a combined movement. The statement of this combined movement is the formula of synthesis which we require.

A brief illustration may make my meaning clear. The history of science in the last century and a half has been of vast importance in the general evolution of society. But the student of society does not need to know, say, the history of the successive analyses and syntheses by which organic chemistry has been built up. What he does want to know is, for example, the way in which the progress of science has affected our view of the world, how it has recast the forms of industry, how it has reacted on literature and art, how it has affected religion and social theory. Again he is interested in the causes affecting the growth of science itself, the effects of political and social liberty, the influence of theological prepossessions, or of the prevailing system of education. In a word, he concerns himself with the place of science in social life, whether as affected by other agencies or affecting them. So regarded, of course, some of the actual achievements of science will interest him. Not only must he recognize the important social bearing of theories like those of organic evolution and therefore take some account of the preliminary scientific work which makes them possible, but he must also note as of transcendent interest the light which scientific progress throws, both by its success and by its limitations, on the power of man over nature. He must, as it were, assess the work of science as one form of human achievement, and one product of the social mind.

As with science, so with other developments of social activity. The detailed history of each affords the data for the sociologist. His special work is to correlate the results.

Again, the formula of synthesis is only applicable when the process which it is to describe forms a unity. But to find this unity in social evolution is no simple matter. In the life of society we are dealing *prima facie* not with one evolution but with many. If, to begin with, we confine ourselves to one nation and try to write its social history, we find two things. First, as already seen, the history tends to break itself up into separate narratives. The religious history of England, say, is something distinct from its scientific, or political, or industrial history. The different evolutions affect and interfere with one another, but yet they have a certain independence. On the other hand, the religious evolution of England could not be understood without reference to that of other countries. Its relation to continental movements of thought is not a whit less intimate than its relation to the remaining phases of social evolution in the country itself. Thus, the social evolution of a country is not an independent unity standing by itself, — it is a part of the wider evolution of civilization.

But here a formidable difficulty arises. When social evolution is taken in this wider sense we may well ask whether any single formula can be applicable to it. When we think of the divergence, I do not say between different European nations, but between the whole trend of Eastern and Western civilization, when we consider the rise and fall of earlier civilizations, when we consider that the existing structure of savage and barbaric society is itself the product of an evolution that if slower in its rate of change has been at work as many centuries as our own, can we say that there is any one single direction which social evolution must take? Must we not rather admit many possible lines of deviation from the primitive center, and speak not of one evolution but of many? Must we not also recognize dissolution as a very serious factor in history, and if so, are we to conceive the evolutionary process as renewing itself, so to say, in an indefinite number of successive attempts, following in a variety of directions where the line of least resistance leads, rather than as a single continuous process advancing in a constant direction? These are among the questions that press for a solution, and their presence gravely complicates our problem. They mean that we cannot start from the conception of social evolution as a unitary process. We must admit divergent lines of evolution. It follows that we cannot reduce the study of social evolution to a simple narrative. Our method must be not so much historical as comparative. It must consist in a review of the multifarious forms of human achievement, with a view to scientific classification.

In this, after all, we are merely following precedent. It would seem that the foundation of any sound evolutionary theory is always a morphology; that is to say, it is a systematic arrangement of the types that we find in accordance with their affinities. Such an arrangement is that which is most likely to throw light upon the actual genesis of successive types, and to prepare us, therefore, both for our descriptive and for our causational conceptions of evolution. In the case of biological evolution, such a morphology underlies the work of Darwin and forms, in fact, the chief strength of his argument. In the famous fourteenth chapter of the "Origin of Species," Darwin points out that though naturalists had not as a rule accepted the theory of descent and had certainly made their classification without regard to any theory of the way in which forms originated, they had, nevertheless, guided by the inherent logic of the facts, arrived at principles of arrangement corresponding accurately to the laws of growth. In their search for deeper affinities, for real resemblances as against superficial analogies, they had come to grouping things together by a kind of logical genealogy which could only be explained when interpreted as a real or physical genealogy. Thus Darwin found the whole fabric of organic evolution standing, as it were, ready waiting for him in the great natural classifications of botany and zoölogy. All he had to do was to supply the connecting link which would show how the species thus arranged into genera, the genera grouped into families, the families into orders, the orders into classes, and the classes into sub-kingdoms, might be conceived as really originating from a common stock in such a way as to generate by intelligible causes those peculiar forms of identity in diversity which constitute the organic world as thus classified. Thus, to link up the organic creation and to transform the dead, crystallized classification into a living movement, Darwin had to do two things. First, he had to show by means of the geological record that the classification corresponded to a real time series, that the simpler forms came first, and that the more highly developed ones succeeded them in due order. To establish this point, so far as it has been established, was the work of paleontology; he had to show, secondly, a means by which the more generic forms would become differentiated into specific types, and this was the special work of Darwin. His method is a classical example of the legitimate as opposed to the illegitimate use of hypothesis. He started from known facts; he began by asking, that is to say, how changes of type are actually produced under our observation, and he found, as he considered, that it was done habitually by human breeders through the accumulation of small variations by selective breeding. He then asked how far the same conditions operate apart from human agency, and he found that the higher rate of elimination of individuals less suited to the conditions of their existence would, for the purposes of his inquiry, have effects analogous to that of the intelligent breeding by human beings. He inferred accordingly that there were conditions permanently at work, which he summed up in the somewhat unfortunately chosen metaphor of Natural Selection, making for the modification of organic types, and he gave reasons for thinking that this agency would, in the main, account for that arrangement of organic forms which was the starting-point of his inquiry.

Now this is a classical example of a good evolutionary hypothesis, but it is easy to see the difficulty of raising such a hypothesis to the rank of a demonstrative truth.

In the first place, it is exceedingly difficult to be sure that the conditions specified in the hypothesis are the only ones at work. That such variations occur was known. That larger variations might occur in the order of nature and be perpetuated by heredity was scarcely suspected. Again, that Natural Selection operates may be taken as an established truth, but that it is the only factor in operation is a very different proposition. Darwin himself thought that it was not, and whether his successors have proved the contrary is still an open question. The problem might be more easily resolved if we could ascertain the second point; that is to say, if we could accurately measure the effect of Natural Selection. Could we determine the limits within which it works, the velocity of the changes produced, and so forth, we could then measure its calculated operation against the observed facts just as Newton measured the calculated effect of gravitation against the observed motions of the planets. But in biology we have as yet no such quantitative laws. Until we can quantify we can hardly demonstrate. All this merely indicates once again that a theory of the conditions of evolution is less easily demonstrated than a theory of the process of evolution.

Now biologists from Darwin's day to our own have been almost exclusively occupied with the theory of conditions. As to what evolution does, whither it tends, what progress it effects, and whether indeed the term "progress" has any application to its works at all, are questions with which they have had little concern. They have been generally content to follow Mr. Spencer in conceiving evolution as a process from the simple to the complex, or they have regarded it simply as a progressive adaptation of the organism to the environment. Only when they have descended into the sociological arena have some of the less cautious among them assumed dogmatically that whatever its direction, evolution is a movement that makes for good and is not to be thwarted by the puny moral consciousness of man. This position, however, we have seen to be not that of scientific biology but of unscientific sociological dogmatism. Of biology as a science it may be said that beyond the generalities mentioned it has not interested itself very greatly in the question what evolves, but almost entirely in the question how things evolve. If indeed we were to put the former question to the biologist, he would reply by referring us to the table of Fauna and Flora with a simple "circumspice." Yet there is a sense in which the question becomes of very real importance, though as we shall see it is quite easy to understand why in this sense it does not interest the biologist itself. If we take any living species and trace its ancestry with the aid of the biologist back to the earliest forms of life, it is clearly open to us to ask, what is the nature of the change that it has undergone? It is also easy to understand that from the biological point of view the inquiry may lead to no very interesting result, and with a few words about differentiation, articulation, and adaptation to environment the matter will be closed. But suppose that the species that we choose is Man, and that we put the question in this way: as compared with the lowest organisms from which we assume him to have originated, what is Man? What distance has he traveled? What powers has he acquired? What is the nature of the changes which have brought this species to the birth? Are they changes of degree or changes which though continuous may yet be called changes of kind? What do they portend? Can we infer from the phases that have been passed through anything as to the future? Can we gain any insight into human potentialities? Can we learn anything of man's ultimate place in nature? It is clear that whatever else may be said of these questions they cannot be dismissed as lacking in interest. But for reasons of which we have seen something the biologist as such cannot answer them, and if he is wise does not meddle with them. But they suggest a way of treating evolutionary problems of which much more will be heard in the future than has been heard hitherto. They suggest the necessity of what I have called a formula of descriptive synthesis, the object of which is to measure the direction and the distance traversed in the evolution of man. By such a measure we arrive at an answer to the question, to put it in a common phrase, of what evolution amounts to. We assess its value. We are able to take a comprehensive and accurate view of what it has done, and we get a firm basis for measuring its further possibilities.

Now the sciences which deal with man from this point of view are two. The first is Comparative Psychology, the second is Sociology. The first is especially concerned with the genesis of the human mind as such. It seeks to determine the stages of development which lead from the first beginnings of psychic life to the emergence of the human reason. It seeks for links to connect what at first sight may appear severed and even disparate, but if it is genuinely scientific, it proceeds without any attempt to slur over differences. In this manner it arrives at a true sense of the distance traveled in the evolution of mind. It has a morphology, too, of its own. The forms in which it is interested are the forms of mental operation, and it seeks to arrange them in such a way as to show how the most elaborate are joined by a series of intermediaries with the most simple. These intermediate phases it finds both in the mind of man itself, where higher and lower operate together, and in various species of the animal world where as it descends the scale it finds the higher functions disappearing one after another.

Now when comparative psychology reaches the mind of man its work is by no means at an end. On the contrary, mental development proceeds even more rapidly than before. But it is now as we have seen a social rather than a mental development, and the psychological becomes a part of the general sociological investigation. Here again the same method is open to us. We can take any phase of civilization, and going back over its ancestry — so far as we know or can reasonably infer it — we can ask what the growth "amounts to." We can inquire into the direction and distance of the social movement which we find. In particular we may do this with our own civilization, necessarily the latest, and actually in many ways a most distinctive and peculiar type. We can go back to what history tells us with certainty, and to what anthropology enables us to infer with reasonable probability of the earlier forms of society, and we can then ask whether, reviewing the life-history of humanity as a whole, we can discover in it under all its wild irregularities, its waves and troughs, its periods of apparent expansion and contraction, any definite and measurable current that has on the whole made a certain assignable distance in a certain assignable direction. When we have discovered this movement we can go on to ask whether it is a movement of progress or not, *i.e.* whether it is one which tends to the realization of ends on which we can reasonably set a value. But first of all we want to know what the movement actually has been. We want to determine the orbit, if orbit there be, of human social evolution. This I take to be the prime object of sociology, and the method by which it is to be approached is a social morphology. Now a social morphology involves not merely a collection of sociological data, but a systematic arrangement of social types, and by social types we mean examples of all the leading forms of human achievement which result from the interaction of individuals, — types of social institution, forms of government, principles of law, types of the family, and, again, intellectual, moral, and artistic traditions, religions, ethical systems, sciences, arts. We need not merely to collect and enumerate the successive achievements of mankind in these various directions, but to arrange them in some way that will exhibit their affinities and interactions, that will help us to appreciate the lines of social development. We need a classification leading up to a social morphology.

Our first business then is to classify, and in its first stage such a classification presents no great logical difficulty. It is comparatively easy, for example, to take an institution like that of human marriage, to run through the data afforded by anthropologists, and by the law books of civilizations, to distinguish certain principal types, and to exhibit other forms as gradations between them. Such a classification is at least more likely to yield positive results than a speculative inquiry into the original form of marriage, which is and must be outside the sphere of possible verification and which can only yield the results which we find by observation, through some more or less ingenious form of historical torture. As against the speculative method which assumes an original type and deduces existing forms therefrom, the evolutionary method regards every type alike as an adaptation of social life to meet certain conditions. Its object is to discover the genetic affinities of these types whereby they pass into one another in response to changes of conditions. The important thing here to discover is what is fundamental and what accidental, and again what is permanent and what modifiable. If this can be done, we may perhaps have a basis for inferring the type which would be found under conditions more primitive than any of which we have a record. But we should not use our suppositions on this point as starting-points for a theory which is to explain the facts. They are rather conclusions, and are likely to be amongst the most doubtful conclusions of the theory already formed.

But this explanation brings to light a real difficulty. We are seeking not merely to classify, but to classify in such a way as to throw light on genesis. That is to say, we want to exhibit institutions in an order in which they might be conceived as growing up. This is what is meant by saying that we want our classification to be a morphology. But it is precisely at this point that logical difficulties arise. For example, we may legitimately classify types of marriage, not upon one basis only, but upon several; each of these will be equally legitimate and the divisions that result will not coincide, but run across one another. Thus we may go by the number of parties to the union, and so distinguish monogamy, polygamy, polyandry, and, if we are satisfied of their existence, group marriage and promiscuity, and between each of these types we may find intervening gradations. But we might equally well group marriages in accordance with the permanence of the relation and distinguish cases in which marriage is indissoluble from those in which divorce is allowed, and divide up the latter again into multitudinous varieties according as the conditions of divorce differ. Equally well we might distinguish marriages by the methods whereby a partner is obtained, as, for example, by capture, by purchase, by service rendered by the husband to the wife's relations, by mutual consent, and so forth. Or, lastly, we might take the relation of husband and wife within the family and exhibit the gradations between the system which gives almost absolute power to the husband and that which leaves husband and wife members of two distinct families and, in the main, independent of each other. How are we to decide which of these possible methods of classification will best bring out the fundamental nature of the institution and of the causes which modify it? There is not — at least there is not yet accepted by sociologists, so far as I am aware — any comprehensive account of the evolution of the family which would explain the rise of all these different forms and bring them systematically into correlation with one another. Here and there, doubtless, we can see certain points of connection. For example, it is easily understood that where a husband purchases a wife from her relations as a quasi chattel, he will have extensive powers over what he has bought. The probability is that his rights will be at a maximum and hers at a minimum, and so we are quite prepared to find wife-purchase associated with a high extension of marital power, with one form or other of polygamy, and with a one-sided system of divorce. But even in such a generalization as this, comparative ethics compels us to be very careful, and this is only a partial and limited generalization covering but a fraction of the facts. It is probable that partial and limited truths of this kind are all that we can attain by studying marriage by itself. Now it is true that we are at present dealing not with explanation but with classification. But we are faced by the fact that we can classify in more than one way, and we want to know which way of classifying will give us most insight, that is to say, which will best express the real affinities of the different types. Now even a cursory study of the facts suggests the truth — and this is the root of the difficulty — that an institution like marriage does not stand alone; its evolution is not an independent evolution. We cannot write its life-history as we can that of an individual physical organism. It is affected by a complex mass of social factors which do not take their origin from the life of the family as such but which impinge upon, and may gradually modify, that life. It is affected, for example, by religious conceptions, by economic conditions, by class or caste distinctions. It is affected, probably, by physiological causes, of the nature of which we are in ignorance, which determine the relative number of the sexes. What is true of marriage is true of any other social institution that we like to take. No one of them stands alone; they impinge, in a degree and manner which can only be learned from experience, upon one another; and modifications in any one of them may thus proceed from without.

It follows that resemblances between different societies may often be what biologists would call analogical rather than morphological. That is to say, though we may find certain features of similarity in institutional forms, this similarity may point to no close relationship, to no filiation, to no real affinity between two societies compared. It is merely what we call — by way of expressing our ignorance — the casual result of a combination of circumstances. The case of marriage itself presents some curious analogical similarities. For example, monogamy is, on the whole, a characteristic of the higher civilizations, but we find sporadic cases of it amongst the lowest savages, and that even in its most extreme form. Indissoluble monogamous marriage is the common property of the Veddahs of Ceylon, one of the rudest races known to anthropology, and of all communities which conform to the law of the Roman Church. It occurs, scattered here and there, among a few other savage tribes, and appears to be contemplated in at least one form of the Brahminic religious code. What real affinity can there be in these cases? There is nothing to suggest mutual influence. There is every reason to deny a fundamental identity of social structure such as would produce a corresponding result. The resemblance is analogical. Conditions, which in some of the instances mentioned are known and in others are not known, have produced a result which is in one respect the same, and that is all that we can say. We cannot use this sameness to draw inferences as to any deeper identity. It is analogical, not morphological.

The same may be said of countless institutions that recur in comparative jurisprudence, or comparative ethics. The equality of a primitive community, for example, has very little beyond the surface fact in common with the equality for which modern democracies strive. The self-government of a village community has perhaps more in common with the representative institutions of a modern state, but yet the differences are probably more important than the resemblances. There is respect for property which is dependent upon a taboo, that is to say, on the belief in certain magical forces which will bring evil upon him who violates it; and there is respect for property which depends upon an ethical appreciation of human rights. In both cases the result is that the property of another is left untouched, but excepting in the result, how little they have in common! These deeper distinctions appear, it will be seen, when we take into consideration not merely the outward form of an institution, but its meaning and value for the society which maintains it. Where outward forms are the same, but the psychological forces that underlie them are different, there is no real kinship. Conversely, where the psychological forces are nearly alike, where the motives or conceptions operating in them are of the same order, there may be considerable differences of external form due to variation of circumstances, but implying no deep-seated divergence of type. If that is so, it is the psychological groundwork that determines the true affinities in a sociological classification. Such, at least, is the hypothesis on which we shall proceed, and it will be at least worth while to see whither it leads us. In practice it will mean only that we must look not merely to the outer form of the institution, but to its principle or spirit. Keeping this caution in view, then, our primary object in the study of social evolution is to distinguish the various phases or forms of social life, whether in the direction of thought or action, of ideas or institutions, in such a way as to obtain a comparative view of the stages or phases of human development, and in particular of that development which has brought a large portion of humanity to the present stage of civilization. When these successive forms or phases are compared, it will become possible to review the movement as a whole and to ask our question — what does it amount to? First, How far and in what direction has it taken us? Second, Does it or does it not conform to our conception of progress?

In a complete survey it is clear that every department of social development would have to be considered — knowledge, imagination, religion, ethics, law, industry, and so forth. Any such treatment within our limits would be out of the question. I can only attempt to illustrate certain aspects of development with the object of showing you how the method may be applied. There are many aspects that attract. I might follow the development of knowledge and the control of life by science, but on this side the conception of progress is familiar and needs little argument to establish its validity. I might deal with the infinitely subtler question of the formation in ethics and religion of principles for the guidance of life, and the emergence of the belief that the well-being of society is itself the ultimate standard to which such conceptions should be referred. But on this side I should be dealing with first principles and with matters that lie beyond our present scope. I shall glance at one point in this development at a later stage, but shall attempt no regular discussion of it. The aspect of development which I propose to take is the elaboration of the principles necessary to social cooperation, and in particular the growth of government and its relation to liberty. These are ideas which lie at the foundation of the social harmony. They belong to the basis of the whole matter, and for this very reason they are at the center of the problems of the present, as of the past. I shall briefly review the main forms of social institution in which these principles are embodied. I shall endeavor to determine in what sense or to what extent progress is to be discovered on this side of social life, and this in turn will lead us to inquire as to the possibilities of progress in the future and the means whereby it may be accomplished.

CHAPTER VI

The Growth of the State

To answer the questions proposed at the end of the last lecture would be to write a book in many volumes. The task of measuring the actual movement of civilization becomes manageable only by a division of labor. I have attempted elsewhere to deal with it from the point of view of ethics, — a point of view which necessarily involves something of the development of religion and something of the development of jurisprudence within its scope. Recently Dr. Müller Lyer, in his "Phasen der Kultur," has applied a similar treatment to the development of industry. Enough has been done to indicate some of the difficulties that beset this method of treatment, and also to suggest certain results. These I will endeavor to indicate to you by taking one side of social life, and tracing development on this side as we pass from the simplest to the most advanced modern societies. As some compensation for the limitations of the inquiry, I will take one of the fundamental problems. I will ask you to consider the nature of the social bond, to examine what is common to all societies and what is distinctive, and I shall try to show that what is distinctive in the nature of the social bond forms a fundamental principle of classification in any social morphology, and serves as one of the measuring rods which helps us to determine the nature of the movement which has made modern civilization what it is. From one point of view, as has been seen, social progress may be regarded as development of the principle of union, order, cooperation, harmony among human beings. This development may be traced in the first instance by means of a classification of the main types of social organization in accordance with the distinctive nature of the social bond.

Now there are, as has been hinted, some forces making for union which are common to the life of all society from the lowest to the highest. There is, for example, a certain mutual interest of a complex kind, which, from the lowest group of savages to the most highly developed civilized structure, tends to keep men together and maintain a certain kind of cooperation. This mutual interest,[1] moreover, is not entirely of a selfish character. It is not only that men have need of one another for mutual defense, or, at a higher stage, for cooperation in industry or in science; there is also the interest in another sense which we take in one another as human beings, and which is a wider thing than sympathy and a less purely moral thing than altruism or unselfishness. The solitary life is, for all but the most exceptional of individuals, the least tolerable of all. We choose — like Alexander Selkirk — "to dwell in the midst of alarms" rather than to reign in a horrible place of solitude. Those we hate are preferable as companions to the desert and the seas. This mutuality of interests, so to speak, is something underlying all human, perhaps even all animal, associa-

[1] Which corresponds, I take it, broadly to what Professor Giddings called the Consciousness of Kind.

tion. It does not therefore serve as a distinguishing principle in social classifications. Doubtless it undergoes changes of degree and even of kind; as society progresses, the interest widens and deepens. On the whole, in the higher societies its more benevolent aspects tend to predominate; but we could not, I think, from these changes of degree make a universal basis of classification.

What we need for our purposes is to find certain principles of union, which serve as bonds for human society, and each of which may at successive stages be regarded as the *leading force* which gives its character to the social union. It is not necessary at a higher stage that the bond operating at a lower should disappear. On the contrary, we shall see that it is still maintained in its own place. But the different forces which I shall distinguish may, I think, be regarded as the dominant forces, each in certain great classes of human society. These forces may be grouped under three main heads, which may be called the leading principles of social union. They are the principles, first, of kinship; secondly, of authority; and thirdly, of citizenship. (It should, of course, at once be explained that a most important bond, distinguished in a way from all these three, is that of a common religion; but it will be seen, as our examination advances, that the element of religion is common to all forms of society, and is to be regarded not so much as a distinct basis of social union, but rather from this point of view as an element involved in the social consciousness itself and as a factor strengthening its hold upon the minds of men.

What, then, are the different forms of society that we find based upon these three main principles? To begin with kinship. The lower forms of society appear to rest in a special way upon the tie of blood, and the way in which this tie is conceived, the extent to which it is recognized, and the manner in which it is extended, whether by fictitious forms or in other ways, gives the key to the social order of the greater part of the uncivilized world. In all the varieties that we find, the one permanent element — as it is, in the order of nature, the most indestructible element — is the relation of mother and children. When some thinkers conceived primitive man as possibly living, isolated, in a state of nature, they forgot one simple and well-established generalization — that all men have mothers; and whatever may be said of the inferior parent, it is at least the universal property of mothers to tend their children, feed, protect, and shelter them as they grow up. This primitive group, which is constituted by the mother and children, runs alike through all forms of primitive and advanced society. It gives rise in the uncivilized world to two main forms of the social structure, which differ in accordance with the position of the husband and father. The husband may form a permanent union with the mother of such a kind that upon marriage a new family group is formed, which will consist not of mother and children alone, but of parents and children. In this case—speaking generally — the position of the father dominates the life of the family; the father remains in his own clan and the wife joins him, and the new group is added to the paternal clan. If we conceive such a family growing up and the sons taking to themselves fresh wives, we can imagine each new family forming a part of the larger household, a family within a family, a part within a whole. We can conceive the grandfather continuing to bear rule, and on his death handing over his authority, perhaps to his eldest son, perhaps to the son pointed out by natural gifts and attainments for the post of honor. If such a stock is fruitful and multiplies, we have a model of the patriarchate, the form of early society familiar to the first anthropological inquirers from the Book of Genesis, from the Roman law, and from what was known of our own Teutonic ancestors. It was a very natural inference to be drawn in the early stage of anthropology that this was in fact the primeval form of human society, but a little further investigation shows that there is another possibility, which has actually been realized over a large part of the earth. The primitive group of mother and children might be formed into a larger society upon a different principle. The connection of husband and wife might be of a less intimate kind. A husband might remain a member of his own clan or of his own group, while the mother and her children remained associated with the group in which she was born; and descent, upon this principle, would continue in the female line, the daughters in their turn obtaining husbands from without, the sons remaining attached to the group, but finding themselves wives in another family. This is the system of maternal kinship in which descent goes, as it is termed, by mother-right. Whether this is the primitive system or not, the evidence is not sufficient to decide, but it is widely diffused in the uncivilized world, and traces of it are to be found in forms, both of civilized and uncivilized society, which have adopted the patriarchate.

The two forms of grouping are permeated by two different conceptions of kinship. In the one, kinship through the female is all-important, and in extreme cases is the only kind of kinship that counts. In the other, kinship through the male is the predominant factor, and kinship through the mother is secondary, is not as a rule reckoned so far and does not carry the same legal consequences. These differences are particularly important in relation to a further development of kinship which is now to be mentioned. It is to be observed that direct descent is not the only form of kinship known either to primitive or to advanced societies. It is certainly conceivable that a single patriarchal family, such as we have first described, might, if it be fruitful and multiply with exceptional success, develop into a clan and even into a large society; but such multiplication could only be very exceptional. In point of fact, another cause of growth has always to be taken into account. Whether kinship be reckoned through one parent alone or through both, it is the almost universal rule that the son or daughter should find a mate from outside the kin, as the kin are reckoned. This is an application of what is known as the principle of exogamy — a principle common to the Chinese, who forbid marriage between all persons of the same name, to the Red Indian, who forbids it to all of the same totem, and to ourselves, who do not allow it within what are known as the "forbidden degrees." Enormously as rules of exogamy differ, the total failure of any prohibition is exceedingly rare, if it is to be found at all, in human society, and the general result of exogamy is clear. It compels a union of distinct families, and in so far as kinship is a basis of cooperation, mutual defense, and so forth, it tends to connect certain families for these purposes. Thus when we speak of kinship as a basis of society we must bear in mind that kinship involves two distinct lines of interconnection — the line of descent and the line of intermarriage. Hence such a society is not limited to one family, but rather implies some association between several stocks.

But limiting, and in a sense counteracting, the rule of exogamy is the hardly less general rule of endogamy, which enjoins marriage within a certain group, and it can easily be seen that while this principle would tend to isolate the group to which it applies, it would equally strengthen the bonds of connection within that group. Endogamy within the clan, for example, would tend to intensify clan life and at the same time tend to separate the clan from the rest of the world. So when the clan develops into a wider society, or when different clans come into association and begin to form a state, the process is frequently marked by a break-down of endogamous rules. In Rome, for example, marriage seems to have been originally limited to the *gens*. Then the patrician *gentes* came together and formed a circle of intermarrying clans, from which the *plebs* was excluded. The *plebs* obtained the *jus connubii* in B.C. 445, and the same right was at an early period extended to the Latins. With the extension of Latin rights, and subsequently of full Roman rights, the possible circle of legal marriage was widened until it included the whole vast Roman world.

So much may be said in common of the principle of kinship, whether it be based on the blood of the father, or of the mother, or of both parents. But there is one important sociological difference between the two cases. Where mother-right prevails, the natural family, that is to say, the union of father, mother, and children, is never complete. The tie between the children and the mother's relations is one thing, and the tie between them and the father and his kin is another thing. The two cut across one another, so that normally under this system the child looks to his maternal relatives for support and protection rather than to his father. So too — as in the case of the Iroquois — the totemic bond cuts across the tribal, and each man is subject, as it were, to two allegiances. It can readily be seen that this does not form so firm a basis for a solid social structure as the paternal family, which makes direct descent always the closest and most substantial relationship and constitutes the natural family a unit, which cannot be dissolved by its relation to other families, though it may count upon these relations for mutual support. Hence it came about that the paternal family yielded the more solid basis for the larger social order of the civilized peoples. But whichever the principle adopted — and there are many gradations between the two, many cases in which elements of father-right and mother-right are blended and which may be regarded as transitional from one system to another — these forms of society resting upon kinship may be regarded as in a sense natural and primitive. They come about in the ordinary course of nature from the family instinct and the successive results which it engenders. We may conceive early society as constituted by ramifications of direct descent and intermarriage from the primordial group of mother and children, the relation of husband and wife being the variable factor giving rise where it is relatively loose to the maternal, where it is closer to the patriarchal system.

The growth of society brings new principles into play. In a primitive group there are, as a rule, few social distinctions. There is generally a leading member or head-man, but the powers of the chief are often but little developed, and are mainly dependent upon his personal prowess. It is true that when the patriarchal clan is highly developed and has grown into a body of many families, acknowledging a common descent from an ancestor who has already become mythical, his eldest male representative begins to wield despotic powers, — as, for example, in a Highland clan, — and his immediate relations, or perhaps his favorites and followers, begin to form a kind of aristocracy. But supposing such a clan, well-organized and disciplined under an ambitious chieftain, to betake itself to a military life, a new order of things comes into play. It will soon find occasion of quarrel with its neighbors — neighbors have a wonderful facility of giving "just" causes of offense to those who are powerful — and the stronger clan starts upon a warlike career. A double series of results ensues. On the one hand, the weaker surrounding peoples are probably reduced to a dependent position. At the lowest stage perhaps their stronger neighbors may merely raid them for their cattle, but as soon as there is some progress in the arts of life their subjection takes a more permanent form. They may become tributary to the conquering people, who continue to live at a distance, or the conquerors may themselves enter into possession of their territory and reduce them either to a feudal vassalage or to slavery, and the distinction of conqueror and conquered will turn into that between lord and slave, or into that of upper and lower caste. Within the conquering people themselves, again, changes occur which affect the whole social order. For successful war discipline is needed, for discipline more powers must be given to the chief. Sometimes in barbaric societies this is pushed so far that the chief becomes absolute master of the persons and property of his subjects. In some of the West African States, like Dahomey and Ashanti, for example, he was the master of the person and property of every man and woman in his dominions. Any man might be made his slave, any woman be taken into his harem. Usually this exaltation of the chief is accompanied and fostered by religious or magical conceptions. The chief is a man-god; his person is sacred; it is even dangerous to his subjects to approach and look upon him. As in Ancient Egypt and in Babylon, his sanctity is carried to such a point that he has to be hedged round by minute ceremonial, his doings intimately affect the fortunes of the people, he becomes responsible for the weather and the crops, and finally, he is hedged in with so many taboos that from being absolute master he becomes a slave— the slave of his own courtiers and the priests; and if he does not manage the weather and the crops aright, it may be the worse for him, not, of course, for his royal spirit — *that* is sacred and immortal — but for the mere body in which it is housed it is another question.

But turning from the religious to the political side of the process, the actual power of a king, it may be observed, is limited by the narrowness of human capacity. The remark is attributed — upon what authority I do not know — to Nicholas I, the most autocratic of the czars, that "Russia was governed by ten thousand clerks." The remark, at any rate, was true, as subsequent czars have probably realized. One man cannot ever govern a great empire. The exceptions of Julius Cæsar and Napoleon exist only to prove the rule, and the greater the empire, the wider the authority, the more it must be delegated. The followers and dependents of the king are naturally favored in the distribution of territory when land is conquered, and they rise to the position of feudal lords, to aspire to some independence where distance tends in their favor. You may remember the story given by Tacitus of the provincial governor who explained to the Emperor Tiberius that it would be better not to raise the question of his removal. He had a large army under his immediate command, and they might (this nominal dependent went on) form a kind of treaty by which the one should be thoroughly loyal and a most obedient subject, but the other should entertain no question of removing him from his command. True or not, this story, dating from the beginnings of the Empire, gives a significant hint of the troubles that recurred throughout the imperial history whenever the hand at the center weakened in its grasp, and which finally led to disruption and decay.

Conquest is originally based on force, but unadulterated force is never a permanent basis of social life.

The ruler must at least clothe himself with the garb of justice or utility. He finds possibly a religious title, whether in the sanctity of his line or in the ordinance of God. In the lower order of such societies, as we have seen, he is himself God, or of the lineage of God, like the Pharaohs. At a higher remove, as with the absolute monarchs of western civilization, he is God's Anointed, he rules by Divine Right. It is rarely the case, as in India, that a priestly caste maintains the supremacy and guarantees the authority of the king, as it were, from above and not from below. But under whatever form, the tendency of this kind of social order is to transmute force into authority. The king governs, it may be, — as in the Chinese theory, — for the good of his subjects, but it is he who knows what is for their good. He is the fountain of justice, the pillar of the social order, the source of every law and ordinance.

The ideas underlying the social fabric are modified in correspondence with this conception. In the primitive community custom was sacred because it was custom, and because of certain sanctions, religious and magical, attending on its violation. In the more elaborate and advanced societies the rule of primitive custom is in some measure broken up. Law is no longer the direct, naïve expression of the popular life. It is in truth at this stage, what some jurists have mistakenly supposed it to be in its essential nature, a command imposed by a superior upon an inferior and enforced by him through the medium of punishment. And it should be understood that the principle of subordination is not confined to the relation of governing and governed; it may run through the whole social life.

We may have a feudal hierarchy of lord and vassal, descending from the king to the lowest subject. We may have a hierarchy of castes, as in India, or we may have an industrial system based on the relation of master and slave, or in the more mitigated form of that of lord and serf, and we may have this principle of subordination maintaining itself in the midst of higher social life in the more or less modified forms familiar to ourselves, in distinctions of class and in conceptions of social, political, or economic inferiority.

At the same time it should be noted that the transmutation of force into authority may have its good side. The absolute monarch may be in fact as well as in name the father of his people. He can often secure a better social order, and even a higher degree of justice, than can be achieved in the primitive society of the kindred. The very fact that he is raised above the body of his subjects may enable him to deal with them impartially; while by the same supremacy he may overcome the discords of nobles, suppress feudal strife, and weld a great people into a single nation. In such a nation there is a sense of solidarity which allows a higher principle to come into being, of which we shall speak a little later on.

But observe first that the authoritarian order has its own moral code, a code which is not perfect, but by no means to be despised. If the superior has privileges, he has also duties. According to the Chinese teachers, the emperor is the last person in the state to be considered. In Ancient Babylon a nobleman, who was tormented by evil spirits, was asked by the exorciser among other things, whether he had done his duty to his dependents, whether he had bound men who should have been free, or left those in prison whom he should have liberated. In Ancient Egypt kings and governors never fail to take credit to themselves in funeral inscriptions for their beneficence and kindness of heart to those whom they had ruled. Of the duties that are inculcated under this head by the higher religions it is needless to speak. All that must be said is that, excellent as these qualities are, they are relative to a social system which creates the necessity for them by its own inherent defects. Benevolence is beautiful, but it is not based on justice, nor is the "Lady Bountiful" the last word of progress in ethics and civilization. Religion and ethics, like government, have their "authoritarian" phase — the phase in which they are conceived as imposed from above and embodied in a hierarchy, and in which their most characteristic teaching is to inculcate the virtues of meekness and obedience on the one side, and on the other gentleness and forbearance in the use of that power which they consecrate with lawful authority.

The Principle of Citizenship

The authority of the superior is not the only method of organizing a large territory and maintaining order and harmony among a large population. There is an alternative known to the civilized, though hardly to the savage and barbarian world, in which the relation of government and governed are in a manner inverted. The people, or at any rate the citizens, are the state. The government is their servant rather than their master, and its members are as much bound by law as the humblest subject of the state. The social bond in this case may often be reinforced by a somewhat vague and extended sense of relationship, by a common language, and by all the complex relations, so difficult to define and analyze, that constitute a common nationality. But the civic bond as such is not the same thing as the link of language or nationality. It consists essentially in a certain reciprocity of obligation as between the individual members of the state, and also as between the state and its members. In some respects the state — to give that name to the social union based on citizenship — resembles the earlier commune. Its government, its laws and customs, come again into close relation with the actual life and character of the people. Law is no longer a command imposed by a superior, but an expression of the will of those who will obey it. So far as the principle of citizenship is carried through, there is a return to a certain equality among members of the state, replacing the hierarchical order of the authoritarian society, and recalling the equality of primitive times. But the resemblances are analogical rather than morphological. There is all the difference in the world between an equality which rests on a recognition of reciprocal obligations overriding preeminence of power, and one which subsists merely because no power has risen to an eminence which could disturb it. There is no less difference between a body of custom which expresses the life and character of a society, — in the sense that it forms the framework subsisting unchanged through ages into which each new generation fits itself automatically, accepting what it finds without question, — and the laws which a changing and developing society makes and remakes with a conscious sense of its needs. There is no less difference between the member of a clan whose rights and responsibilities are fixed by his place in the clan and the individual who can shape his own life and whose rights and responsibilities are determined principally by his own actions and agreements. The fully responsible individual, on the one side, and the legislative government expressing the will of the majority, on the other, are the characteristics of the state.

Now the principle of citizenship may be carried out with very varying degrees of thoroughness. It is complicated by questions of kinship, race, and nationality, and it is in practice blended in greater or lesser degree with the principle of authority. Further, the life of the state depends a good deal on the area which it covers, and is gravely affected by its external relations. These considerations go far to determine the actual character, the forms, and the life of the state as we see them in history. The earliest form of the state known to us is the city state of ancient Greece. Here the typical state was a fortified town of moderate and often of very small dimensions according to our standards, occupying a strong position in a strip of territory belonging to and cultivated by its citizens. But even in this small community the principle of citizenship was not pushed through. In most states a considerable part of the population were either slaves, as at Athens, or formed a servile caste like the Helots at Sparta, and whatever rights were secured to the slaves by law, custom, or religion, they were certainly in no sense citizens.

So far the despotic principle remained vigorous and living within the system of the free community. But in many states there were further gradations among the free men themselves. There were close oligarchies, like those of Thebes and Sparta, to whose members alone the privileges of government were confined, while the rest of the population, though personally free, like the Spartan Periœci, or the Roman plebs, were citizens only in the passive sense. Yet we should not deny the name of state to these oligarchical republics. The difference that separated them from the slave-holding democracy of Athens was more one of degree than of principle. The circle of the aristocracy formed internally a true state, but a state which had dependents which it governed despotically. The breaking down of class barriers and the extension of political and civic rights which makes up a large part of the history of Athens, of Rome, and of modern European nations is simply a development of the principle of citizenship at the expense of the principle of authority, until ideally it is extended to all permanent residents in the territory.

The city state of the ancients proved incapable of expansion. Democratic Athens governed her short-lived empire with reckless despotism, and the jealousies and resentments which she excited ruined the noblest city of Greece. The extension of the Roman suffrage as Rome consolidated her conquest was a beneficent admission of a wide circle to civic rights, but reduced the constitutional machinery of Rome to a farce. Citizens from all parts of Italy could not meet in the forum to elect consuls or pass a law, and the representative method was not thought of till the Republic was already dead. I will not speak here of the mediæval city states, with their checkered but often glorious history, but will pass at once to the country states of the modern world, and will confine myself to noting two points of difference. Through the principle of representation, and often aided by the consolidation previously effected by an absolute monarchy, the modern state has largely solved the problem of uniting large areas and great populations on the basis of common citizenship; and owing to the disappearance of slavery and serfdom among white peoples has had no such sharp demarcations of free and unfree to overcome. Hence within its borders the principle of citizenship is in a fair way to be carried to its conclusion. Yet the old problems revive it in a new form. On the one hand, modern economic conditions engender inequalities of wealth and foster forms of industrial organization which constantly threaten to reduce political and civic equality to a meaningless form of words. On the other hand, within its borders the state through its very size finds itself frequently confronted with problems of race and nationality, which sometimes threaten its fundamental principles, while without it is usually encumbered with dependencies, to which it seldom scruples to add when occasion serves. Of the economic problems I shall speak later, but on the question of dependencies and of nationality a word must be said as bearing directly on the principles of government.

The conquest of a territory by force and its retention without regard to the wishes of the inhabitants is of course in flat contradiction with all the principles of citizenship. The democratic state which sends an autocratic governor to rule a great dependency is employing two distinct methods of rule, one for use at home, the other for use abroad. My own country may be regarded internally as a qualified democracy. The British Empire as a whole is as much an oligarchy as Sparta. The Indians are its Periœci, and perhaps the Kaffirs its Helots. The government of white people by this method has, however, been abandoned. It was virtually destroyed by the American Revolution, and the renewed experiment in this direction may be said to have been brought to a conclusion when autonomy was extended to the Transvaal and the Orange Colony. The despotic principle tends now to coincide with the color line, and much of the future of the modern state, particularly of my own country, must depend on the relation of the white to the colored and non-European races. Until the rise of Japan as a modern power, it was almost universally believed that the characteristics of European civilization were a monopoly of race, and that whether we liked it or not, non-European peoples were forever destined to a type of civilization and a form of government totally different from ours. Probably the greatest social change now in progress in the world is the rise of a new spirit in the East which altogether repudiates this view, and the reaction of these changes upon the West will, I am convinced, if met in a statesmanlike spirit, be bracing and beneficial. We are not, however, concerned with speculation as to the future. We have only to note the fact that as it stands the principle of citizenship is crossed in the empire states of our own time with that of the authoritative government of dependencies, and that this fact has important reaction on our own domestic constitution. We cannot deny principles of liberty to Orientals, or for that matter to Zulus, and yet maintain them with the same fervor and conviction for the benefit of any one who may be oppressed among ourselves. We cannot foster a great bureaucratic class without being impregnated at home by its views of government. We cannot protect a great dependency from without except by remaining a great military and naval power; and to all these necessities our own body social must accommodate itself.

Mutatis mutandis, the same remarks apply to the foreign relations of the modern state. More and more, as means of communication multiply, the fate of each state is bound up with that of others, and the attitude of hostility still characteristic of the modern world threatens the healthy internal development of each member of the community of nations. If a nation may sometimes be consolidated by fear of an aggressor, it is consolidated as an armed camp, and its military organization tends to bring it back to the authoritarian form; the taxable resources of the community are expended on the means of defense or aggression; and the interests of the public are diverted from the improvement of social relations, not by wars, but by ever-renewed rumors of war. On this side, then, the development of the civic principle seems bound up with internationalism, and with a readjustment in the great empires of the relation of governing state and dependencies.

Within the state is apt to arise the even more difficult problem of nationality. It is in this form that the principle of kinship is mainly to be reckoned with as a political force in the modern world. Nationality, indeed, is not properly a matter of race. Most of the bodies of people which feel themselves to be nations are of highly complex racial origin. Yet the sentiment of nationality is confessedly analogous to that of kinship: it is a natural unity stronger in the fact than in the logical analysis, a composite effect of language, tradition, religion, and manners which makes certain people feel themselves at one with each other and apart from the rest of the world. Pride and self-respect are closely bound up with it, and to destroy a nationality is in a degree to wound the pride and lower the manhood of those who adhere to it. Analyze it away as we may, it remains a great force, and those states which are rooted in national unity have in them a great living power which will carry them through much adversity. But few states are fortunate enough to be one in nationality, and the problem of dealing with the minority nation is the hardest that statesmen have to solve. Clearly it is not achieved by equality of franchise. The smaller nationality does not merely want equal rights with others. It stands out for a certain life of its own. The endeavor to suppress it ends invariably in the withholding of some of the general civic rights which are fundamental to the state system, and in this sense unreconciled nationalities are a standing danger to the civic principle. To find the place for national rights within the unity of the state, to give scope to national differences without destroying the organization of a life which has somehow to be lived in common, is therefore the problem which the modern state has to solve if it is to maintain itself. It has not only to generalize the common rights of citizenship as applied to individuals, but to make room for diversity and give scope for collective sentiments which in a measure conflict with one another. How far it will succeed is again matter of speculation, and as such beyond the subject of our immediate inquiry, the object of which is merely to indicate to what extent the principle of citizenship has in fact been carried in the modern world and what are its principal limitations.

If we put together the heads of this necessarily rough sketch, we can, I think, trace the lines of a significant development. At the basis we have the ties of kinship engendering the close association of the small local group and at a higher stage of the firmly knit clan, within the somewhat larger but looser unity of the tribe. Such associations may have much vital force, compactness, and endurance, but they are narrow and in proportion to their strength tend to be hard, self-contained, and mutually hostile. They are, moreover, adapted only to rude economic conditions and a rudimentary condition of the arts of life. Hence, they yield with advancing civilization to the rule of force by which, in the guise of kingly authority, far larger aggregations of men can be held together and a more regular order can be maintained. In this change there is loss and gain, gain in the development of order, loss in the suppression of much that is essential to humanity. On the other hand, the principle of citizenship renders possible a form of union as vital, as organic, as the clan and as wide as the empire, while it adds a measure of freedom to the constituent parts and an elasticity to the whole which are peculiarly its own. Further, when pushed to its conclusion, it reveals the possibility of a world state in which the constituent groups, as well as the constituent individuals, would have legitimate scope for self-development. To say that such a state is actually in the making would be rather to give utterance to a sanguine view than to rehearse the indubitable facts which are the subject matter of science. But to say that the modern world as it stands affords the conditions rendering such a state possible, and that there are important factors in the social mind working towards it is to keep within the limit of fact. Now we cannot say of humanity as a whole that it began with the system of kinship, passed into that of authority, and ended with that of citizenship. At most this might be said of certain societies, and of these the civic societies of antiquity lost their preëminence and fell into decay. What we can say is that the system of kinship is dominant in the lower and earlier stages of culture, that the system of authority is characteristic of the advance towards civilization, and that of citizenship of the higher civilization. It is, of course, possible that the civic systems of the present day may decay like those of antiquity, but taking it as it stands, the characteristic modern state, with all its imperfections, exhibits the most complete reconciliation yet achieved on the large scale of social cooperation with the freedom and spontaneity of the component individuals, localities, and nationalities.

CHAPTER VII

Evolution and Progress

The evolution of the state sufficiently illustrates the general character of the movement with which we have to deal, and the difficulties which it presents to the inquirer who seeks to determine its direction and extent. On the one hand, the movement is not direct, but eminently tortuous. This in two ways. Even if it were true that humanity as a whole, or every distinct human society, passed through the three phases that have been distinguished, it would be impossible to conceive the development as the working out of a single principle. On the contrary, the order and the extension introduced by the principles of force and authority tend to cancel and obliterate much that is distinctive and vital in the simpler life of clan and commune, while the principle of citizenship is opposed in fundamentals to that of force. The utmost that can be said is that the civic state can in its fullest and widest development make a synthesis of the elements contributed to social life by the earlier forms of organization, and can make use of them for its own ends and subject to the control of the ethical conceptions on which it rests. So far, we might conceive the modern state as emerging out of earlier forms by a union of elements which in them were divided and therefore one-sided. But we could not possibly ascribe such a synthesis to any inherent historic tendency in the nature of society as such. For we find no regularity in the matter. Many societies have never advanced beyond the principle of kinship; many others remain organized on an authoritarian basis. The state has come into existence several times, and in very different forms, and has seldom if ever been based on the pure principle of citizenship consistently applied. There is not, in fact, one movement, but many movements, and these impinge on one another, sometimes perhaps to reinforce one another, but more often to deflect or even to cancel. The utmost we can say of the whole is that when all is summed up there has been a resultant movement which has in fact given us the modern state as the dominant type of society in the dominant peoples of the modern world.

But this does not end the matter. The modern state is not a fixed and crystallized type, exhibiting a single principle of construction consistently carried through. On the contrary, our account of it could not be carried beyond the most elementary abstractions without reference to a host of unsettled questions. The state as we know it is not a solution, but a problem, not a fixed point that has been attained, but a movement. Its history ends for us in a question. This question, moreover, involves a philosophy, and that alone would explain why the study of the facts in sociology forces us, even against our will, into philosophical inquiries.

Now if we were to take other departments of social evolution, we should find very similar results. Suppose, for example, we were to take the idea of justice, and consider it first on the side of the treatment of the offender. We should find the idea of suppression operating in a few exceptional cases from a very early stage, and extending itself in close connection with the growth of the principle of authority into a theory of punishment, tending to become more severe and even more brutal as the social order consolidates itself, but finally beginning to yield to principles of prevention and cure as the authoritarian conception gives way to that of common citizenship. Side by side with this line of development, we should find the idea of retaliation, at first distinct from that of suppression, and then blending with it to sharpen the point of vindictiveness in punishment, and then again confined within the limits of compensation or restitution. Once again the history, by no means simple or straightforward in itself, would end in the imperfectly solved problems of criminology. Or we might take justice in its other and milder aspect, as the means of maintaining right and redressing wrong; and here we should note how redress from being a matter for the injured individual, becomes a concern of the kindred and the clan, and finally of the impartial authority of law and government. So far the element of progress is sufficiently clear. But if we turn to the question what rights society acknowledges and enforces, we should come once again on great irregularities of development. The equality of primitive society gives place to a hierarchical subordination as the authoritarian principle develops, while this again yields to a reëstablishment of equal rights in correlation with the principle of citizenship. But, once again, we should end in a series of questions. What does equality mean? Is it a logically coherent, practically workable conception? How is it to be defined, and is it in effect realized under modern conditions?

Thus the actual movement of society is both irregular

and incomplete. It yields no assured social harmony. The question is whether it does, upon the whole, tend to realize the conditions out of which when complete a harmony would emerge. Is there among the changes that we note a gradual evolution of these conditions, or is an advance in one respect, at one period or in one society, balanced by losses in other respects, at other periods or in other societies? The answer is not simple, but upon the whole it is in one respect negative and in another positive. Progress so conceived is not continuous, but within the area covered by our investigation it is real, and in fact fundamental.

Thus, if we compare the first and last terms of the series, we recognize a series of changes of fundamental importance for the advancement of true social cooperation. We note first the extension of order, the widening of the social unit from the primitive local group outwards, until for certain purposes it begins to extend itself to the whole of mankind. We note next the increased firmness and solidity of this order, the evolution of impartial justice, which is the basis of all healthy social union, and its extension till it grasps the whole of the community under a common rule. We find the conception of a common life advanced by the destruction of the manifold forms of group morality, giving place to the principle of full membership of the extended community for all who dwell within its borders. We find at the same time a more liberal provision for the free movement and spontaneous effort of the constituent parts of the community, giving concrete reality to the principle that the most stable order is that which is based upon freedom. We find a more general enforcement of mutual forbearance, combined with a wider and richer development of mutual aid. Such are some of the results which strike us when we compare the highest with the lowest terms of our series. When we look at the intermediate terms, we see that the process of advance is not simple and continuous. We have repeatedly seen that development in one direction has entailed arrest in another. We have seen, for example, that the familiar antithesis between order and liberty is not wholly destitute of historical justification. We have seen that the rise and extension of authority might destroy much of the rude vigor of a simple community, or at a later stage extinguish the light of civic freedom. Similarly we can see how the maintenance of order may be secured by harshness of procedure and cruelty in punishment. We can see how the growth of society may foster inequality and depress the position of those who do its manual work; at the same time we can see how with the growth of the social mind there comes a conscious effort to rectify these evils. We see in a word, that, while certain essential conditions of harmony have been realized, the problem as a whole has not been solved. The work of progress is on every side unfinished. It is not a crystallized product, but something left in solution.

By extending our investigations very similar results could be shown to obtain over a wide range of human activity in thought, in religion, in law, in ethics, in politics, and in industry. We cannot say that each institution passes continuously from lower to higher phases. We can say that at each point in the range of survey we find forms implying a germinal condition of the social mind, and forms implying the relative maturity of the social mind; we can say that the low forms coexist in the societies which appear nearest to the primitive type of human life, and that in the characteristic modern societies, notwithstanding all imperfections, the highest types coexist, some in maturity, others in process of formation. We can show that, while at certain stages there is opposition between one condition of development and another, — which is a chief cause of the irregularity which we find, — in the long run and at a greater depth there is harmony, and this harmony asserts itself the more as the development of the social mind proceeds. We are thus able at once to understand the slowness and uncertainty of social progress and to establish the conception of its ultimate reality, on the level, at any rate of a hypothesis which conforms to a wide range of fact.

I must not now attempt to cover this range in detail. Our time will be better occupied with the further consideration of the problems that have already emerged. But I must glance for a moment at the development of knowledge and thought. This development, observe, is essentially a social phenomenon, depending as it does on the power of each generation to make use of the accumulated results of its predecessors. And as its causes are social, so also are its effects. It is from our present point of view simply the effective and essential psychological basis of the intelligent direction of life. This result is most obvious in its bearing on industrial development, where we readily trace the steps, becoming larger and more rapid as they proceed, towards the subdual of external and physical conditions to human needs. But in the deeper regions of thought and philosophy and in religion we can point to a corresponding development less easy to formulate in terms which will avoid all controversy, but not on that account less significant. The comparative study of ethico-religious thought reveals an inner movement that corresponds in the main with the more outward changes and institutions which have been sketched, and justifies us in referring them not to changes of outward circumstance, but to the genuine growth of social mind. It shows how the vital impulse of human thought on this side becomes at once more personal and more social, more personal in that it is recognized that both religion and ethics must be spontaneous and self-chosen if they are to be sincere, more social in that the ideal of life and duty which they uphold comes to be more and more consciously dominated by the conception of the individual as a member and a servant of the single society of mankind. On this side, in fact, comparative investigation bears witness to a gradual revaluation by which the social import of action and of character, from being an unrecognized and indirect condition, emerges into the position of the acknowledged ultimate standard of our judgments of what is good or bad, right or wrong. The full discussion of this development would lead us into fundamental questions which lie beyond our limits. I will only say this much. The turning-point in the evolution of thought, as I conceive it, is reached when the conception of the development of humanity enters into explicit consciousness as the directing principle of human endeavor, and, in proportion as the phrase is adequately understood, is seen to include within it the sum of human purpose in all its manifold variety. In particular, it can be seen to be the conception necessary to give consistency and unity of aim to the vastly increased power of controlling the conditions, external and internal, of life, which the advance of knowledge is constantly yielding to mankind.

With regard to the interpretation of historic progress, then, our case stands thus. On the one hand, we have traced in the history of institutions the gradual realization of the conditions fundamental to true and full social cooperation. On the other hand, in the history of thought we can trace the extension of the rational control of life leading up to the conception of the social development of humanity as the guiding principle of effort. But if this is so, we have arrived at a point where the devious lines of social progress converge, and that is the point at which they become united by entering into the consciousness of mankind. If we put the question, "What is the actual result of historic progress?" the answer is in outline sufficiently clear. Progress has consisted in the realization of the conditions of full social cooperation and in the extension of the rational control of life. But the whole of the advance actually realized now assumes the aspect of a merely preparatory stage. For it culminates, as its lines converge, not in a sense of completeness, but in the formation of a purpose — the purpose of carrying forward consciously and unswervingly that which has gone on in unconscious, broken, and halting fashion, the harmonious development of the social life of mankind.

This result enables us to deal with a problem of the first importance to sociological method, and that is why I have been obliged to refer to it here in a fashion so cursory as to do little justice to its value. To understand the problem, we may suppose a critic to argue in this way. "I will grant you," he may say, "for the sake of argument, that you have established a certain measure of social progress as a realized fact. But what does it prove? You have by no means shown that progress is the law of life. On the contrary, by your own admission, it is not even continuous within the area that you have examined. It comes in occasional spurts, succeeded by epochs of stagnation and decay, and if, on the whole, the successive spurts have carried modern society a little further than earlier societies, what is this to teach us as to the future? You yourself draw a clear distinction between the trend of evolution as an observable fact and a law of evolution resting on the permanent conditions of social life. The results of your comparative investigation may have given us the former, but they cannot yield the latter, which is what we really want to know. You also yourself distinguished the question of fact from the question of value. You showed that to prove that society has moved or is moving on certain lines is nothing to the point if we would wish to know whether it is desirable that society should move on certain lines. How, then, does the comparative method serve us? If it neither teaches us what ought to be nor what will be, is it of any use beyond the justification of a speculative curiosity?" It is very important to come to an understanding on this point. It affects our whole attitude to the teaching of history, to the study of contemporary movements, and to the method of sociological investigation. It will determine whether our method is to be inductive or deductive, whether it is to be analytical or historical, whether it is to be guided primarily by ethical conceptions or a study of empirical facts, or whether it is to combine these various methods, and if so in what way.

Now the most succinct form of answer that can be propounded may be put in this way. The study of actual evolution in the past does not suffice to tell us with certainty either what ought to be or what will be, but it tells us what may be. The reply emerges from the results of the investigation itself. For if our account is correct, it exhibits the social mind as gradually arriving at the point of self-determination, that is to say, at the point at which it becomes master of the conditions internal and external of its own movement. But if this is so, two results follow. On the one hand, if conditions which in the past have dominated the development of mankind can be intelligently controlled, they will no longer dominate it in the same way. A new and revolutionary factor has been introduced, and the course of events in the future will be *pro tanto* unlike the course of events in the past. On the other hand, the general conditions of progress, though controllable, are still operative. Man is not free to make of himself whatever he pleases. The artist who works on a given material may have perfect mastery of his material, but it is a part of his mastery to know what can and what cannot be done with it. Similarly, if we suppose the most perfect insight into social conditions and the most complete control over them, the result will be simply the most perfect understanding of what we can and of what we cannot do. In particular we want to know whether the social mind can so operate upon the conditions of its existence as to secure a more complete harmony. On this point our comparative inquiry gives us the best materials for a decision. It shows us, if we are right in our conclusions, that when all is said and done, the progress made in realizing the conditions of such harmony is real and substantial. It shows also that the conditions of further progress are present. That is to say, it removes the preliminary doubt whether permanent social progress is a genuine possibility in the nature of things. Such a doubt is only too forcibly suggested by many of the undeniable facts of human history, and of the contemporary world. It is impossible to shut our eyes to the long periods of stagnation and retrogression that make up a great part of recorded history. The optimism which sees in the declining ages of the Lower Empire and amid the barbaric anarchy of the Merovingian period nothing but the birth of a higher order does not represent the balanced mood of science. Real loss, deep-seated injury long in the repairing was involved in the break-up of the Roman state, as earlier in the destruction of Greek freedom and later in the decay of the mediæval city. No doubt each of these forms of social organization perished through inherent defects, and the order which followed upon them had virtues of its own. By laying stress only on the faults of the perishing and the good side of the new, we can nurse an optimistic belief in continuous and inevitable progress. But it is equally open to another, who prefers to nourish a more melancholy mood, to make a reverse selection and contemplate the tendencies to corruption and failure inherent in human affairs. But in sociology more than anywhere else the difference between the scientific and the rhetorical, sentimental, or popular mode of treatment consists precisely in the endeavor to look at things as a whole and therefore to give due thought to all sides, to gain as well as to loss, to loss as well as to gain. From such a view, — applied as dispassionately as possible throughout the field of human society as revealed by anthropological inquiry into the condition of uncivilized people, — and by the historical record of civilization, two results appear to me to stand out with sufficient clearness. The first is negative. The theory of continuous automatic inevitable progress is impossible. Assuming that progress means an advance towards an ideal that would commend itself to a rational judgment of value, it is impossible to maintain that the successive steps which lead from savagery to the civilization of our own day involve point by point a corresponding betterment in the actual life of the people as a whole. The slave or the serf of the middle civilization compares unfavorably with the free savage, and even the low-grade worker of our own days does not in all respects come happily out of the comparison. Without any trace of rhetorical exaggeration or of sentimental idealization of so-called natural conditions, we must admit a real and grave loss in certain elements of value when we compare the relative concreteness and human interest of the primitive hunter's life with the mechanical drudgery of the routine of unskilled modern labor. Moreover, even if it were true that every onward step in civilization taken by itself were net gain, it would still be untrue to suppose that humanity as a whole had always gone forward in civilization. The advance has been greater than the retrogression, but there has been true retrogression as well. Free Athens did not perish without leaving the world the poorer.

Much was saved from the wreck, but the loss was real, not to be ignored.

So far the negative view. The positive result that emerges is that once again, when we take the same comprehensive survey and give full weight to all the considerations that have just been glanced at, the advance is real, and what is more, it is of a kind to prove the possibility of a far more substantial and unchallengeable advance in the future. For the substance of the advance consists precisely in the evolution of a higher and more comprehensive social mind, and when this is taken as the central fact of human progress, all history appears, in Comte's phrase, as a preparatory period. It is the record of the growth of mind to the stage of unity and self-consciousness necessary to give it the mastery in its own house. So regarded, the history of the social mind takes its place as the latest, but not by any means the last chapter in the still larger history of mental evolution in general, the process by which mind emerged from rudimentary beginnings in the lower organisms to the central position which it occupies in the life of the human individual. As comparative morphology traces the growth of the eye from a pigment fleck sensitive to photo-chemical stimulation to the complex organic structure which ranges earth and heaven, so the comparative psychologist traces mind from the first stirrings of uneasy feeling prompting physical readjustments to unpleasant stimulus to the mind that ranges the circle of reality; and the social psychologist completes the work by tracing the building up of that far larger unity to which the mind of the individual is related as a cell to the brain.

Now in this view of development the halting, broken, and uneven nature of progress becomes readily intelligible. The control of mind is at first very limited. The animal and the primitive human being are for the most part the sport of natural conditions. It is *a priori* probable that the more advanced type should be swept away over and over again by physical cataclysms, by the superior brute strength of lower animals, or by the mere fecundity of noxious micro-organisms of the lowest type, in a word, by natural selection. Such catastrophes would be most common at the lowest stages; and in fact, long geological periods passed before the higher types of animal made good their footing upon the earth. Primitive man was subject to fundamentally similar conditions, and we may well believe that the slow advances which we trace through the vast extent of the Paleolithic period were constantly frustrated by the survival of the unfit. If the men of the reindeer period, who drew the mammoth, and with roughly pointed flints carved the horse on bone to the admiration of our ethnologists, disappeared entirely from Europe, they only met the fate which has over and over again befallen the higher type. The victory is not to the best, but to the strongest, and it is not till the best becomes the strongest that it can secure the permanence of its type. But in proportion as the social mind grows, the sphere of its control expands. One by one it becomes master of conditions which previously held it in thraldom. It is progressively less liable to destruction, and the epochs of history grow shorter. In the uncertainty of geological measurements it is useless to speak in terms of thousands or tens of thousands of years, but the Neolithic period is admittedly of short duration compared with the successive stages of the Paleolithic epoch, and the ancient Oriental civilizations are again short-lived in comparison. Yet they too were subject to successive deluges of barbarism. The Hellenic civilization, with all its wonderful achievement, was nothing but a tiny islet in a world of far lower culture; and the greatest gift of the ruder but more robust Roman to the world lay in this, that he was civilized enough to recognize Hellenic superiority. Against the massive influences of barbarization both within and without the imperial frontiers the best elements of the Greco-Roman culture maintained a long but losing fight, and the modern history of the West represents a new movement which had the advantage of starting with many vital elements of the old culture preserved through the wreck. The distinguishing characteristics of our time are that civilization for the first time has the upper hand, that the physical conditions of life have come and are rapidly coming more and more within human control, and that at least the foundations have been laid of a social order which would render possible a permanent and unbroken development.

The progress of mind in its lower stages is not arrested by external enemies alone. On the contrary, its own limitations engender diseases which entail arrest, decay, and possible dissolution. The very growth of control over external nature is the root of social inequality. If not its first, it is its sustaining cause. The individual, the caste, the race of higher powers will hold the weaker enslaved to their immediate profit, to the gain of industrial civilization, but to the immeasurable loss of much beside. The mechanical developments of the eighteenth and nineteenth centuries afford the basis, as I would contend, for a wholly new type of civilization, but this possibility is not to close our eyes to the lowering of the standard of life and the mechanizing of great masses of human beings which they have entailed. We may go still further, and maintain with Plato that in the civilized world every form of society perishes by its inherent vices as much as by external assault. Thus, the states of Plato's own time decayed through internal faction, and the narrowness of the spirit of autonomy which forever nipped the shoots of Pan-Hellenic sentiment. The Roman state, enjoying a far higher level of political capacity, could not reconcile liberty with empire, nor even the stability of automatic rule with the power of the soldier and the vast physical extent of the frontiers. For the modern world there remain problems of reconciliation no less grave, and the question which must be answered before our view of the comparative security of modern civilization can be finally established is just whether the social thought of our day is sufficiently advanced to solve them. At this point once more the theory of social evolution ends in the demand for a social philosophy.

If you have followed me so far, you will readily apprehend my general answer to the criticisms which I suggested. The aim of comparative sociology is to measure the actual achievement of social progress, and its result is to indicate the attainment of certain fundamental conditions of harmonious development by the maturing of the social mind on many different sides and through numerous assignable phases. This result (1) does not enable us to infer a mechanically inevitable continuance of the social movement in any particular department on the lines of the past or of the present, because, if its version of the facts is correct, new factors are coming into existence whereby social history becomes less and less a matter of mechanical necessity and more and more controlled by purposive intelligence. Nor (2) does the history of social progress as such afford a sufficient basis for the social philosophy which it postulates, for such a philosophy consists not in the record of past movements, but in the effort to form a rational and comprehensive purpose to guide the future. None the less the inductive theory of evolution lies at the back of any sound social philosophy, for it is to this theory that we must look for proof that in philosophizing we are not merely beating the air. It is this theory which goes to show that the development of the social mind is a reality; that its growth is the condition of progressive harmony; that it is where its control of the conditions fails that progress halts; that the sphere of its control is upon the whole greater in our own day than at any previous time; and that it has in fine advanced far enough to show that the possibility of a harmonious development of human life is no dream dissolved by the cold touch of physical science, but a reality to which the entire story of evolution, physical, biological, mental, and social leads up. ∴

CHAPTER VIII

SOCIAL PHILOSOPHY AND MODERN PROBLEMS

WE have said that the history of social evolution ends on every side not in a solution, but in a problem, or if we prefer so to put it, that the solutions so far attained only give rise to fresh problems. This being so, the case for progress rests at bottom on the belief, justified as we suggest by a comprehensive view of a wide range of fact, that we have reached a point at which it is becoming possible to solve the problems of social life by the deliberate application of rational methods of control. But this statement suggests conclusions which will not pass unchallenged. It suggests, for example, an extension of collective action which some will regard as inimical to the liberty, the individual enterprise, the personal initiative which they have been accustomed to regard as the mainspring of whatever progress the world may have seen. And going back to our account of the state, they may bring some of our own arguments to aid their case. For our account tended to show among other things that what differentiated the modern state from earlier forms of society was the increased regard for personal right, for equal justice, for all that is summed up in the conception of Liberty. Here, then, in the relation of the individual to the state we come upon one of the greatest of the unsolved problems and we may fairly be asked to put our social philosophy to the test by inquiring whether it has any help to give in the solution.

Let us first see how the problem has shaped itself to modern thought. It is no novel difficulty. Ever since I have known anything of political controversy in my own country the question of the just limits of the action of the state on the one side and the liberty of the individual on the other has been matter of lively controversy. It is a point on which the movement of democratic opinion in particular has been irregular, and has been and still is a cause of perplexity to many persons of strong humanitarian sympathies. The older school of English Liberals and Radicals were in general for restricting the sphere of the state. This is true not only of the Manchester School, to whom national liberty was the center of all things social and political, but, on the whole, of the Benthamites also, whose utilitarian creed was capable of a quite opposed interpretation. Nor was the tendency to restriction peculiar to the Radicals. In its degree it affected men of all parties. It was the temper of the period from 1832 to 1886. In our own time the position is reversed. It is the democratic element in politics that urges the development of state activity. If we hear protests on behalf of the liberty of the individual, it is generally from the lips of some one who is resisting change. Nevertheless this modification of view is not peculiar to a single party. There is a general shifting of the balance. The democratic elements have gone furthest, but the whole of society has gone a long way with them. It is generally recognized that the sphere of public responsibility has been enlarged and has to be still further enlarged. The reluctance to assign new functions to the state is a diminishing quantity.

The extension of the sphere of common responsibility

may be seen first in the remarkable growth of public control over industrial contracts, arising in the first instance out of actual experience of the working of unrestrained competition. The material prosperity brought about by the industrial revolution which began to take effect towards the close of the eighteenth century was soon seen to bring a host of new problems in its train. Of these the employment of young children was most pressing, and, notwithstanding the predominance of the *laissez-faire* principle, an exception had to be made in the case of juvenile labor at an early date. But in the case of children all but the most rigid adherents of *laissez-faire* were ready to make exceptions. It was clear that children of six or seven could not be regarded as self-determining agents; they could make no bargain on their own account; and to regulate the conditions of their work was not to interfere with the contract made by the worker, but at worst with the contract made by the parent or the guardian of the worker, and as, in the case of child labor, the guardian was very often no one more nearly connected with the child than a Poor Law official, the case for natural liberty was not a very strong one. The question of women's labor was more difficult, and there have been those, from Mill to some of the champions of feminine equality at the present day, who have stoutly maintained that no restrictions should be imposed upon women that were not equally binding upon men. This, however, has not been the generally accepted view. It has been more commonly held that women workers were economically in too weak a position to protect themselves, and that in safeguarding them

the state was not to be regarded as interfering with the
natural liberty of the fully responsible individual, but
rather as exercising a duty of tutelage over a class of
persons unable adequately to protect their own interests.
Be this as it may, the employment of women and children
in factories gave rise in my own country to a series of acts
of continually increasing stringency for the regulation of
the conditions of their employment. As long, however,
as the ideas of *laissez-faire* prevailed, such regulations
were regarded as exceptional. They were justified only by
the economic dependence of the person for whose benefit
they were instituted; they dealt only with certain conditions of labor considered to be necessary for health.
They did not profess to regulate the whole of the bargain,
for they never touched wages; and though indirectly
they did restrict the employment of the male worker,
they did not do so professedly or of deliberate intention.
In our own time we have seen a great extension of the
principle in these two respects. The hours of the adult
male worker have been brought under the regulation of
a government department in the case of the railways,
and, after a prolonged controversy, the hours of miners
have been closely limited by law. The Miners' Act has
special significance in this respect, as it was the point
upon which the battle of trade-union versus political
action was fought out, both among the trade-unionists
themselves and in the wider arena of public controversy.
But in recent years the British government has even
gone further. It has followed the example of the
Australian and New Zealand legislation, and has under-
taken to deal not only with the regulation of hours and
sanitary conditions, but, in the case of certain selected

sweated industries, with the rate of wages itself. That is to say, a legally recognized authority undertakes to control the entire bargain made by the worker with his or her employer in the industries concerned. Once again the special ground taken on behalf of the trades in question is the economic helplessness of the worker. But once again we have a principle laid down clearly capable of very wide extension. Though the action of the wages boards is confined to a very small number of selected trades, there are tendencies at work which make indirectly for a very much wider extension of public supervision. The great organized industries have come more and more to trust to collective bargains between employers and employed, arrived at by conciliation boards consisting of equal representatives of both sides, meeting as a rule under the presidency of an impartial chairman; and where these boards fail there is a growing tendency on the part of the public to demand the intervention of the Board of Trade. Though neither capital nor labor would at present desire or agree to compulsory arbitration, it becomes year by year more difficult for either party to refuse on demand to submit its case to an impartial tribunal.

In such ways as these the ground is being prepared for a far wider extension of public responsibility in the matter of industrial regulation. If from the regulation of industry we turn to the provision for poverty, we see an analogous change in public opinion. The Poor Law Commission of 1834 was dominated by the desire to restrict public assistance within the narrowest possible limits. Unwise and irregular forms of pecuniary aid had done much to pauperize the poorer classes, particularly in the rural districts, and experience in this instance told heavily on the side of theory as against public intervention. The Poor Law Commissioners clearly conceived that the problem of the pauper was in essentials a problem of idleness, and that to cure pauperism the prime necessity was to stimulate industry and thrift. There seems to have been little question at that time but that a man who would work could find work and work sufficient to support him and a normal family in normal circumstances. Provision for the poor should on this view be required only in cases of disablement, childhood, sickness, or overwhelming misfortune. Such cases could in large measure be left to private charity, and where this failed the state should come in, it was thought, only where there was complete destitution, and the test of real destitution was willingness to submit to the restrictions of the workhouse as a condition of the receipt of relief. Now the actual history of industry since 1834 has shown that some of these assumptions can no longer be maintained. With regard to the fundamental question of employment, for example, the facts have clearly shown that the case is far more complex. Unemployment is due to very various causes; the character, ability, and physique of the worker together undoubtedly constitute one of them, but as undoubtedly this is not the only one. The actual volume of employment is subject to seasonal and to longer periodical fluctuations, and in times of depression the statistical evidence is clear that large numbers of respectable and hard-working men are thrown out of work through no fault of their own.

More accurate information on these and on many

other causes and incidents of poverty are no doubt largely responsible for the change of opinion. The sweeping character of this change is illustrated by the present movement for the break-up of the Poor Law. The Commission, which issued its report in 1909 was, unfortunately, not unanimous. The majority adhered in the main to the older view, though with a liberal and progressive interpretation; but an important minority, whose work has met with a very wide response from public opinion, took up an entirely different line. Their object is to eliminate the test of destitution altogether as a condition of relief. They urge that to watch a family sinking by degrees into the depths and to wait until it touches bottom before a hand is held out to help it is neither humane nor economical. They say that the process is most easily arrested at the beginning, and instead of public relief to be resorted to as a painful and most undesirable form of cure when the evil is done, what is required is rather public assistance to act as a preventive. Instead of seeking to restrict public aid, therefore, within the narrowest possible limits by imposing a more rigid test of destitution, they would rather encourage the coöperation of the individual with the public authority. They look on public assistance rather as a good than as an evil, of which men should be encouraged to avail themselves rather than dissuaded from resorting to it. They are not unaware that such a principle might be so misapplied as to weaken the necessary stimulus to personal effort, and they seek to overcome this difficulty by suggesting more efficient arrangements for the recovery of the cost of public assistance from those individuals who benefit by it and are in a position to pay for it. Whether this machinery is or is not adequate is a practical question of great difficulty which will have to be very seriously discussed; but for the moment I am concerned merely to illustrate the evolution of opinion, and I could hardly take anything more significant than the change from the conception of relief as a necessity to be kept within the narrowest possible limits by imposing the test of destitution, to the conception of public assistance as a normal incident of life, from which society and the individual may alike be the gainers, and which rests at bottom not on principles of regulated charity, but rather on those of a reciprocal right and duty. Nor is the new principle merely the watchword of a party. It has in substance gained legislative recognition. From our present point of view perhaps the most startling departure from old traditions taken by the British legislature in recent times is to be found in the Old Age Pensions Act of 1908; and what is most remarkable about this act, when considered as an evidence of the movement of opinion, is that it was in substance a non-party measure; both sides freely claimed credit for the initiation of the idea and for the support given to the concrete proposals of the Liberal Government. Criticism and opposition were indeed heard, but they proceeded from a resolute few who gathered together as a forlorn hope around the standard of older economic convictions, but who, so far as their effect upon public opinion was concerned, were voices crying in the wilderness. The act of 1908 completely threw over the principle of destitution as the basis of a claim to public assistance. It awarded a pension of 5s. a week to all men and women of seventy and upwards in the enjoyment of an income of less than £21 a year each,[1] provided that they were British subjects and that they fulfilled certain elementary conditions of industry and respectability. There was, indeed, one provision reminiscent of the older views: persons who should have received poor relief subsequently to the 1st of January, 1908, were to be disqualified from the receipt of a pension; but this pauper disqualification, as it was called, at once encountered severe criticism, and it was only maintained in the original act on the plea that financial considerations made it impossible further to increase the number of pensioners at the outset, and by the incorporation in the act of words providing for the surcease of the disqualification on January 1, 1911. The disqualification has accordingly lapsed with time, and from the beginning of this year the pension has in fact been available for all persons of respectable standing of the age of seventy within the income limit, unless they are actually compelled to resort to a Poor Law institution by failing to find friends who can take care of them outside. The fundamental character of this change in our system for the relief of the aged has hardly yet received all the emphasis which it deserves. The tendency of people who introduce a great change in a conservative country like England is to minimize the departure from precedent; but in reality the breach with the past is great, and probably irreparable. The test of destitution disappears; nor in reality is any other substantial test, as of character, industry, or thrift, substituted for it. All proposals of such a tendency encountered strong opposition, and

[1] Above this income the pension diminishes on a sliding scale till at the limit of £31. 10s. it is extinguished.

were in time whittled away to a bare minimum. The principle implied by the new law is at bottom no other than this: that the bulk of the people are so circumstanced that they cannot be expected to make adequate provision for their old age unaided, and that it is accordingly the duty, as it is within the power, of the community to provide the bare minimum necessary to an independent life. It is very instructive to consider the arguments used against and in favor of this contention. As against the pension system, it is urged, in accordance with the older view, that it is the business of the individual to provide for himself, and that, where the parent has failed to do so, it becomes the duty of the child to support him or her. To this it is replied, as already hinted, that the burden upon the individual was too great to be borne; that the children would, by the time their parents attained the age of seventy, be themselves as a rule responsible for a family or for other dependents; that in practice it was found impossible to obtain from them the support that was desired; that they would in reality do more for their parents if the pension were there as a basis to go upon; that the old folks, instead of being left to drift into the workhouse, would be honored and welcome guests by the fireside, and that for the individual the motives to thrift would not be weakened nor the springs of industrial activity broken by the provision of a bare minimum, to which every one would find it highly desirable to add what he could by his own efforts. It was contended that men did not save for old age because they could not hope to lay by enough to secure for them independence, nor even means of subsistence as comfortable as was provided in the workhouse; but that, if they could count on so small a sum as 5s. a week, they would try to add to it another 1s. or 2s. or half-a-crown. It was urged, therefore, that, so far from paralyzing, it would tend to stimulate thrift, so far from superseding, it would tend to rekindle the dying embers of filial responsibility. When it was urged that men should at least contribute to the provision for their old age, it was replied that the scanty earnings of a workman were better devoted to the objects of immediate necessity for the health and efficiency of his family and himself; and that, if the contributions were to be anything more than a sham, the requirement would, in fact, wreck the value of a universal scheme which would relieve the Poor Law of its greatest burden.

As between these two lines of argument, the facts must decide; experience must show whether in point of fact the springs of industry are weakened, whether thrift diminishes, whether the family tie is loosened, whether self-respect is undermined. Hitherto none of these evils have been apparent, and though, in the length of time that has elapsed, there has not been sufficient evidence for the formation of any decided opinion, there can be no doubt that public opinion as a whole has acquiesced in the Old Age Pensions Act of 1908.

One of the arguments in favor of old age pensions is based on the consideration that they give help at a time when the recipient has become helpless; but old age is, of course, not the only period of helplessness. There are for the poor, and indeed for all of us, properly considered, the years of childhood, when we are wholly dependent on others; there are the risks of sickness and mutilation by accident; there is the period of incipient old age, when sickness passes into permanent invalidity; and finally, for the working people, there is the recurrent risk of unemployment. Now for all these risks public remedies have either been provided or are being actively canvassed and urged upon government by important sections of public opinion. By the act of 1906 the application of the money of ratepayers to the feeding of necessitous children in schools was permitted, though the adoption of the act was left to the decision of the local authority. With regard to sickness and invalidity, a scheme of insurance is now before Parliament following upon the lines of the German model and involving at least a substantial provision on the part of the state. With regard to unemployment, the question is one of infinite complexity, and no solution can as yet be regarded as anything but experimental. But the responsibility of the state is more and more clearly recognized. As soon as the figures of unemployment begin to mount up, whether from seasonal causes or owing to periodical depression, there is at once a demand for the public provision of work, and, experience having shown the exceedingly unsatisfactory character of regular relief works, this has tended of late years to take the form of the pushing forward of the ordinary municipal works that are actually required on public grounds in the locality, and the endeavor so to arrange them as to make the period of greatest municipal activity coincide with the times of industrial depression. One of the recommendations of the minority of the Poor Law Commissioners is that this method should be extended so as to form a regular scheme. As the waves of expansion and depression extend roughly over a period of about ten years it is proposed, so far as possible, that public works should be laid out in advance upon a ten-years' scheme with a view to dovetailing the expansion of municipal and governmental employment into the depressions of ordinary industry. It is suggested that a figure of about £4,000,000 a year represents the difference between the wages paid in good and those paid in bad years, and that an expenditure of about that amount will go far towards equalizing the fluctuation of the labor market and saving the workman from the anxieties and disasters attendant upon failure to obtain employment. This proposal in itself constitutes a considerable advance in the direction of the public organization and control of the labor market, but it does not stand alone. It is recognized that no such effort would cover all cases, and it is proposed in addition that there should be an assisted scheme of insurance against unemployment, whether working upon the model which Continental experience has made familiar, of subventions to trade-unions or other friendly societies which already give benefit to their unemployed members, or by a new state system, which would be universal and compulsory.[1]

I need not now discuss the rival merits of these two proposals; I only note both alike involve the principle of largely increased public subvention to the needs of poverty,—involve, in other words, the acceptance by the state of responsibility for a large measure of the risks which the workman has hitherto borne unaided. Beyond this we have the proposal, also urged by the Minority Commissioners, that the labor exchanges,

[1] Both schemes are in fact incorporated in the Bill now before Parliament.

themselves constituting a new state agency for the provision of employment, should be constituted the center of a machine by which no adult healthy working man or woman would be left without means of support in periods of industrial crises. The machinery of the labor exchange, it is suggested, will when sufficiently perfected suffice to determine whether there is or whether there is not a real shortage of labor. It will become possible to say of any individual whether he is out of work through his own fault or not, whether he has declined reasonable offers, whether he has lost employment through some defect of his own, or whether he is there in attendance at the exchange ready and able to give efficient service but unable to find the man he is to serve. When thus the sheep are parted from the goats, it is said, it will be possible to deal with both classes. The determined idler must not be allowed to prey upon society, he must not go cadging about for odds and ends of useless jobs or for bits of charity; he must not be allowed to keep his wife and children in rags, ill-housed and underfed. The children must be cared for; the mother, if she is doing her duty by them, is doing one woman's work and may fairly claim public maintenance with no possible question of a return. As to the man, he is a fit subject for discipline and restraint. For him a labor colony must be provided, where he must learn to work and gain his discharge as soon as he can prove himself efficient enough in mind and body to stand the stress of industrial competition. On the other hand, for the willing worker who can find no means of maintenance, there must in justice be a different order of treatment. He will have to be maintained, occupation will have to be found for him. It is suggested that if no directly productive occupation can be found, a system of industrial training would be possible, and in this way, among other objects, the means would be provided of bridging over the trade transitions, which are another cause of economic distress. Up to middle life, at any rate, men who are being ousted by a new process might either learn that process or acquire some skill in an alternative occupation. Now, I cannot do justice to these proposals on their practical side within the limits of this bare sketch, and I must ask you not to judge of their practicality from the brief references which I have made. I do not suggest that they are all of equal value, or that they need be adopted or rejected wholesale. I mention them to illustrate the trend of opinion, to show you the forces which are at work in England, to enable you to understand the direction in which they are taking us, and to measure the rapidity with which the sphere of collective responsiblity for the welfare of the individual is being extended from year to year.

The period under review has witnessed an equally remarkable extension of the functions of the state as the organizer of certain great departments of life. The most conspicuous of these is public education. Within the lifetime of men who still survive the function of the state in education was conceived as being adequately discharged by the grant of a few thousands a year in support of voluntary societies for the better education of the poor. Within my own lifetime the state has made itself responsible for the elementary education of three fourths of the community, and from elementary education it has advanced to secondary education and at least to an active interest in and a modest financial support of education of a University type. Here again the older liberty of the family is impaired by the principle of compulsion, while what earlier thinkers would have regarded as a necessary incident of parental responsibility is taken on to the shoulders of the public by the remission of fees. No more striking illustration of the extension of state functions could be given than a comparison of the budget of an Education Minister of the present day with that of 1850 or 1860.

But it is not to be supposed that the extension of state control is indiscriminate, nor is it to be inferred that the essentials of personal liberty have undergone such restrictions as might appear from a bare recital of the facts to which I have referred. If we look to other sides of the national life we see no such movement. There is in England an Established Church and, though it would be true to say that the movement for Disestablishment in England has made comparatively little headway during the last generation, it would be impossible to find any counter movement that is seriously to be reckoned with. On the contrary, the period which I have had under review has witnessed the Disestablishment of the Irish Church and a lively and determined agitation for the Disestablishment of the English Church in Wales; while if we look again to the case of education, we see that whereas in all secular matters the increased authority of the state is welcomed on all sides, the smallest attempt to impose anything that can be regarded as a state religion arouses the quickest suspicions and is combated with the fiercest resentment. The contrast may suggest that the true interpretation of the modern movement is not to be reached by setting up an abstract opposition between state interference on the one hand and the liberty of the individual on the other; the question at stake is as to the kind of liberty which shall be left to the individual and the kind of responsibility that falls to the community. On this question the thinkers of our time, and particularly the great democratic thinkers, take a view very different from that which prevailed in the days of Cobden and Bright. It does not follow that they value liberty less, though it may perhaps be true that they trust to government more. We may carry the discussion further by looking a little into the causes of the change of attitude which I have endeavored briefly to describe.

The intervention of the state in the sphere of economics may be ascribed in the first place very largely to the sheer teaching of experience. Palpable evils resulted from the régime of free contract, and humane men took the only apparent means at hand for combating them. This cause by itself, however, though it might suffice to explain the Factory and Mines Acts, would not cover the whole of the field. Looking a little deeper we see an intelligible reason for a far-reaching change of attitude on the part of democratic thinkers toward the state in the series of political changes which have converted the government from an oligarchic constitution to one in which the will of the majority can, at least when it is sufficiently resolute and united, obtain its way. The government which the men of

Bentham's day criticized was something too nearly resembling a close and corrupt corporation; it was not distinguished for competence, it was not remarkable for an enlightened and disinterested view of public questions. The prejudice had sunk deep in the minds of reflecting men that the government conducted no business efficiently, and was seldom to be trusted to attempt such conduct with a single eye to the common weal. The reform of the Civil Service, which has given us probity and efficiency of administration, and the extension of the suffrage, which has given to the mass of the male population the last word on public issues, has necessarily altered the position. The modern writer, if he sympathizes with democratic aims, looks at government as a machine which may be used to embody his views and give them legal effect. He has overcome his distrust, he has found that efficiency is possible, and he has come to assume honesty and integrity almost as a matter of course.

Political changes, then, which have given us constitutional democracy, have paved the way for what, if the term were not limited to a rather narrow theory, we might call a social democracy, what we may at any rate call a democracy seeking, by the organized expression of the collective will, to remodel society in accordance with humanitarian sentiment. Here we touch a third and still deeper cause which must be brought into the account. The period which we have reviewed has witnessed a progressive deepening of humanitarian feeling and of the sense of collective responsibility. The public mind will no longer acquiesce in the sweater's den any more than it would acquiesce in this country sixty years ago in negro slavery. Here we touch a feeling which is not the peculiar privilege of any party, but which is, in its degree, common to all classes, which inspires voluntary effort no less than political agitation, and which underlies not merely the Liberal and Radical legislation of the last five years, but also in its degree the Tariff Reform movement, which is the leading proposal of the Conservative or Unionist party. On all sides men are agreed that problems of poverty, problems of education, problems of physical, mental, and moral efficiency, are matters not merely of individual and private but equally of public and governmental concern. They do not deny the duty or depreciate the responsibility of the individual for himself or of the parent for his family, but they superimpose upon these a duty of the citizen to the state and a responsibility of the state for the individual.

Upon the whole, then, we find that if the change of attitude has been sufficiently sweeping it is not altogether indiscriminate. There is a great extension of collective activity, but it does not seem to be attended by a vital loss in the sense of personal freedom. It remains, however, to inquire further whether the two things are at bottom compatible, or whether by advancing farther on the one line we must in the end retreat upon the other. This is the question propounded by the actual movement of opinion to our social philosophy.

CHAPTER IX

THE INDIVIDUAL AND THE STATE

OUR task to-day is to examine the movement of opinion which has been outlined, in the light of social theory. We held that social progress consists in a harmonious development, and we further defined this conception as including a harmony in the development of the personal life of the members of society, and in the working out and fulfilment of the various and at first sight divergent elements of value which constitute the wellbeing of the social order. In the movement of opinion we have seen a certain conflict of ideals and our question is whether, if we probe deeper, a basis of reconstruction can be found. To find an answer let us take up the question afresh. Let us start with the conception of the social order which the principle of harmonious development would suggest. Let us consider to what view of the functions of the state and the rights of the individual it would lead and let us, in order to observe the limitations of time, deal with the question with special reference to the problem of liberty.

To begin with, the general theory of society indicated by the ideal of harmonious development is clearly one of coöperation. We may say, with Aristotle, that society is an association of human beings with a view to the good life. The social life is essentially a coöperation in the working out of common objects, and the best organized society will be that in which the coöperation is most perfect and complete; but in saying this, two distinctions have to be kept in view. In the first place coöperation has its negative as well as its positive side. Mutual aid is essential to social life; mutual forbearance is equally necessary; indeed, as a condition of living together, at least of living a harmonious life together, it is even the more fundamental of the two, and also perhaps the more difficult to secure. In thinking, then, of social life as a form of coöperation we must lay stress not only upon the activities which it cultivates in common, but on the idiosyncrasies which it tolerates, the privacy which it allows, the divergent developments of personality which it fosters.

Secondly, in speaking of the ideal of society, we must remember that social life and the life of the state are not one and the same thing. From the principle that social life is a mode of coöperation we cannot infer offhand that the function of the state is to foster coöperation of the same kind and in the same degree. To determine what functions the state itself has to perform within the coöperative social life, we have to ask ourselves, first, what are the special characteristics of the state as a form of society, and how these special characteristics affect its function. Two characteristics which affect all state action occur to us at once as bearing upon the question of its legitimate sphere. These are, in the first place, that the life of the state is crystallized into the form of definite institutions, that its ordinances have to be incorporated in laws and rules of universal application, that it must deal with men in masses and with problems in accordance with what is general and not with what is particular. Hence it is with difficulty adapted to the individuality of life; it is a clumsy instrument, as it were, for handling human variation. It is inadequate, to adapt Bacon's phrase, to the subtlety of human nature. Its sphere is the normal, the prosaic, the commonplace; its business is to solidify the substructure of society rather than to pursue its adornment. It can handle the matters upon which ordinary people usually agree better than those upon which there is variety of opinion.

In the second place, the state is a compulsory form of association. Its laws have force behind them, and not only so, but the state does not leave it open to the inhabitants of its territory to decide whether they will remain members of the association or not. In a voluntary association there are rules compulsory upon all those who remain members, but the ultimate liberty is reserved to individuals to part from the association if they please. In the case of the state, this ultimate liberty can only be exercised by quitting the state territory altogether, and even that privilege has been at various times denied to the subjects of the community, and is to-day not unhampered with difficulties for the poor. Now it is true that there are important functions which the state can perform without the direct use of compulsion. When government conducts a business enterprise it does not necessarily compel any one to avail himself of its services, nor does it necessarily suppress competition. On this side the question as between the state and the individual is not one of the limits of liberty, but of responsibility.[1] But ordinarily

[1] See page 201.

the intervention of the state action does involve some sort of compulsion upon the individual and in what follows we will confine our attention to cases of this kind. It is not difficult to see that functions may be useful and salutary when freely performed which would be useless and even injurious when imposed on reluctant people. In a sense this may be said to be true of all moral and spiritual functions in so far as they are moral and spiritual, because when performed under compulsion they lose their moral and spiritual value. It is not to be inferred from this that the state has no moral or spiritual functions. Indeed, its action in certain capacities may be one way, and possibly the best way, of expressing the moral and spiritual interests of its members. It does suggest that its action as a spiritual body can only have value in as far as it is expressing the will of its members, and not imposing a law upon them which they do not freely and voluntarily accept.

It follows further that the legitimate functions of the state must depend upon the whole circumstances of the society which is under consideration. The kind of compulsion that is necessary, the degree of success with which compulsion can be applied, and the reflex consequences of its employment upon the general life of society will depend essentially upon the composition of the community and the relation of the government to its subjects. For example, in a very homogeneous society, where all the people are of one race, one allegiance, and one religion, there will be a general adherence to the same customs, a general sympathy with the same ideals of life, and there will be little difficulty in maintaining laws which could only be imposed upon an alien race by means of extreme severity. In such a society, then, the sphere of the state can quite usefully be extended to functions which, in a complex empire governing men of different nationalities and rival religions, will produce confusion and the breaking-up of laws. One cannot, then, lay down general rules as to the functions of the state which will apply to all times and places. Our only general rule will be that, seeing that the state is a form of association and is limited by the fact that its functions have to be crystallized in definite institutions, expressed in universal laws and in large measure carried out by the use of compulsion, their sphere must be determined by considering how far the objects of social coöperation can be furthered by methods of this kind, or how far, on the other hand, the nature of the methods necessary will itself conflict with the ends desired.

In this discussion we have said nothing as yet of the rights of the individual as such, or of the ideal of liberty as itself a fundamental barrier to certain kinds of state action. In fact, this antithesis between the rights of the individual and the welfare of the state, between liberty as such and restraint as such, appears to be a false antithesis. To begin with, if liberty is a social conception, there can be no liberty without social restraint. For any one person, indeed, there might be a maximum of liberty if all social restraints were removed. Where physical strength alone prevails the strongest man has unlimited liberty to do what he likes with the weaker; but clearly, the greater the freedom of the strong man the less the freedom of the weaker. What we mean by liberty as a social conception is a right to be shared by all members of society, and very little consideration suffices to show that, in the absence of restraints enforced on and accepted by all members of a society, the liberty of some must involve the oppression of others. Just as the liberty of the strong man to assail the weak destroys the liberty of the weak man to call his body his own, so — to take an instance from our own contemporary experience — the liberty of the motor-car to use the roads may, and often does, go so far as to impair the liberty of any other class of vehicle or the liberty of pedestrians to use the same road for their purposes. Excess of liberty contradicts itself. In short, there is no such thing; there is only liberty for one and restraint for another. If liberty then be regarded as a social ideal, the problem of establishing liberty must be a problem of organizing restraints; and thus the conception of a liberty which is to set an entire people free from its government appears to be a self-contradictory ideal. Like other contradictory ideals, it has in fact an historical explanation. A community as a whole may cherish the ideal of freedom, and by freedom may mean escape from the whole system of government under which it lives, when that system of government is imposed by an alien power. Thus a subject nationality or a subject class may claim freedom in a quite general sense, but it is freedom, if properly understood, not from government altogether but from alien government, not from law as such, but from the particular laws alien to the good of the subject people, which are imposed upon them from without. In a self-governing people, unless the machinery of democracy is very sadly out of gear, so complete a want of touch between governing and governed can hardly be apprehended. Law and government in such a case must in the main express the character, on the whole forward the collective purpose of at least the majority of the individuals constituting the community. And here arises an important corollary to what has been said above of the ethical basis of state functions. So far as self-government is genuinely realized, state action expresses the combined will of individuals. The desires of the individual citizen may effectuate themselves most fully through state machinery, and in so far as the law and the administration are carrying out the moral will of the majority, so far their action has just as much moral value as though it were performed by the individuals themselves through the agency of a voluntary association. Hence when we trace the growing confidence in state action to the advance of democratic institutions we touch a deeper principle than that of the mere political control of the legislative and administrative machine. As long as law could be fairly regarded as a rule imposed by a superior there was a serious meaning in the antithesis between that which the law did for people and that which people did for themselves. There was point in the demand for self help and the voluntary organization of mutual aid as something intrinsically superior to the parental interference of a superior authority. There was a ground for saying that the former method fostered a manly independence and a "living" sense of social responsibility, while the latter was a species of charity which might sap these qualities. But when the reform of the law depends on the deliberate resolve of the people themselves, when it is won at the cost of a hard-fought political struggle, by the appeal to reason, by a contest involving widespread earnestness, some self-sacrifice, much serious attention to some social problem and the means of solving it, then the law is no magician's wand helping people out of trouble with no effort of their own. It is the reward of effort. It is the expression of a general resolve. It embodies a collective sense of responsibility. It is, in a word, something that a mass of people have achieved by their combined efforts for their common ends, just as a well-organized trade-union or a friendly society is an achievement won by combined effort for common ends. Now this, it may be objected, is an idealized picture of the working of democracy, and I am far from ignoring the seamier side. Nevertheless in so far as popular government succeeds, it does realize some elements of this ideal, and just so far the older objection to the extension of the sphere of the law which rests on the danger of weakening the moral fiber loses its strength.

But we can carry the argument a step further. If liberty is among other things the right of self-expression, this is a right which masses of men may claim when they want the same thing. Majorities will claim it as well as minorities, and they will seek to use the means that lie to hand for effectuating their claim. Now it may be that legal machinery is the only efficient means for the purpose, and if the members of a majority are debarred from the use of such machinery, their will is to that extent frustrated and their right so far denied. Now there may be good grounds for this denial. It may be better that a majority should be prevented in any given instance from exercising its will. The objections to the use of coercion in some directions may be, and for my part I should agree that they are, so great that it is better that the majority should fail to get its way. But do not let us shut our eyes to the fact that to insist on this in any case, whether for good and sufficient or for bad and insufficient reasons, is alike to put a restraint on self-expression, and to that extent upon liberty. The liberty of the minority in such a case is (as always) a restraint upon the majority.

Two questions, it will be seen, arise from this discussion. The first is, what are those matters in which the majority can only find self-expression through the machinery of law? The second is, what are those considerations which may legitimately restrain the majority from exercising their power even when as a result their *prima facie* right of self-expression is defeated.

The reply to the first question is in principle simple enough. Experience shows us that there are many things that can be done by individual initiative and by voluntary association, but that there are also many things in which these two agencies fail. A man may worship God as his own feelings dictate without compelling others to worship with him. He may associate himself with those who are like-minded. He may form a church where all may worship together after the fashion upon which they are agreed; and their worship, if it is a worship in spirit and in truth, is none the less hearty, none the less spiritually effective because of the existence of others who frequent different churches or who frequent no church at all. The effective formation of religious organization then does not depend upon universal adhesion, and in carrying out their common will, the members of a church have not to depend on securing the coöperation of those who differ from them. Hence, for this reason if for no other, the religious life of a community may be pursued with vigor without calling on the state for support.

On the other hand, there are many cases in which coöperation, if not universal, is altogether ineffective. Take, as an instance, the question of the early closing of shops. The great majority of employers in a given district may desire to close early, both for their own sake and for the good of those in their employment; but, as every one knows, in the world of competition the refusal of a handful of men, and perhaps even of a single tradesman, to agree to the common desire may wreck the whole intention. Unless the minority can be compelled to come in, the majority cannot get their way. In such case it would seem that an end, which the community holds valuable and which the majority of those affected by it desire, is a fair subject for enforcement by the common law with its compulsory powers.

Again, paradoxical as it seems at first sight, it is nevertheless profoundly true that there are cases in which the interest not of one man only or of some men, but of all considered individually and temporarily, is opposed to the interest of all considered collectively and permanently. Thus it is the interest of any individual at any moment to buy what he wants as cheaply as he can. But it is quite possible that a system of free competition catering for the temporary needs of each individual purchaser should have the effect of gradually and imperceptibly lowering the standard of production by substituting cheapness for quality. If so, the process set up by each man following his immediate interest may result in a general deterioration of standard whereby in the end the interest of each is less effectively served. Nor can the individual stand alone against this process by exercising a more far-sighted view. He cannot resist the tendency set in motion and constantly propelled by the pressure of immediate interests. It is only concerted action that is effective against the pressure of the mass, and if by such action a higher standard of quality can be permanently maintained, all are in the end the gainers. To take a slightly different illustration: any man driving a motor-car wants to get on as quickly as he can. The same man when walking may be annoyed or endangered by the speed of other peoples' cars, but by driving carefully himself he cannot force others to do the same. He can secure his safety only by supporting legislative and general control. Once again: it may be the interest of any particular employer to buy labor as cheaply as possible. He cannot, unless he has exceptional organizing capacity, pay more than others. But it is not to the interest of employers as a whole that the classes from whom their work-people are drawn should deteriorate in efficiency and lose in purchasing power through low wages and bad industrial conditions. Hence collectively they may be ready to accept regulations which individually they would be powerless to put in force.

The principal sphere of the state then appears to be in securing those common ends in which uniformity or, more generally, concerted action, is necessary.

On the other hand, purposes which can be secured without compelling the adhesion of those who do not accept them fall naturally within the sphere of individual enterprise and voluntary coöperation. The function of the state then is to secure the common ends which recommend themselves to the general will and which cannot be secured without compulsion. But at this point our second question emerges: Is the general will, supposing that its ends cannot be secured without compulsion, to be entirely unfettered, or are there some general considerations which might still exercise a restraint in favor of the liberty of the individual?

This brings us to the question on what that liberty is based. We have seen that each man's liberty involves a restraint upon others, and we are asked to conceive it now as a restraint upon society as a whole. On what grounds is this restraint to be justified? In ordinary phraseology, it would depend upon the rights of the individual, and we have here to ask what is meant by a right. A right is generally said to be the correlative of a duty. If I have a right against you, you have some duty towards me. The duty may be quite general and purely negative in its character. For instance, I have a right to walk along the street without being pushed off the pavement into the mud, and your duty is merely to give me reasonable room. But, whether general or special, we may agree that the rights and duties of citizens form together a system making up as a whole the moral order recognized by society. In this order each duty is, broadly speaking, that which is expected of the individual; and each right is that which the individual expects of some other person or of society at large. Generically, therefore, a right is a kind of expectation; but it is not only an expectation, but an expectation held to be justified; and the important question is, on what grounds this justification is based. In the first place, it may be a legal right, and the justification then lies in an appeal to law. But, in addition, there are, or there may be, rights which the law does not recognize and which the moral consciousness holds ought to be recognized. These are the moral or ethical rights of men. The older thinkers spoke of them as "natural rights," but to this phrase, if uncritically used, there is the grave objection that it suggests that such rights are independent of society, whereas, if our arguments hold, there is no moral order independent of society and therefore no rights which, apart from the social consciousness, would be recognized at all. Our analysis of the term "right" goes to show that a right is nothing but an expectation which will appeal to an impartial person. A may make a claim on B, and B may refuse the claim. The claim only becomes recognized as a right if some impartial third person (C) upholds A in making it, and on what ground can C as an impartial being base his judgment? As impartial, he is looking at A and B just as two persons equally members of the community with himself. If there exists a rule recognized by the community which covers the case, no question arises. But we are looking at the case in which no rule exists, and C has to frame his decision on first principles. To what in such a case can he look except the common good? If he maintains as a right a general principle of action incompatible with the good of the community, he must hold that what is right is one thing and what is good another, and that not merely by the accidental circumstances of a peculiar case but as a matter of principle. Unless then we are to suppose such deep-seated conflict in the ethical order we must regard the common good as the foundation of all personal rights. If that is so, the rights of man are those expectations which the common good justify him in entertaining, and we may even admit that there are natural rights of man if we conceive the common good as resting upon certain elementary conditions affecting the life of society, which hold good whether people recognize them or not. Natural rights, in that case, are those expectations which it would be well for a society to guarantee to its members, whether it does or does not actually guarantee them. If this view is accorded, the more developed the conception of the common good the more completely will a society guarantee the natural rights of its individual members. To extend the conception of the rights of the individual will be one of the objects of statesmanship; to define and maintain the rights of its members will be the ever extending function of government.

Any genuine right then is one of the conditions of social welfare, and the conception of harmonious development suggests that there will be many such conditions governing the various sides of social life. If so the general conception of harmony implies that these conditions, properly understood, must mutually define and limit one another; not only so, it implies that in proportion as they are properly understood they will be found not to conflict with one another but to support and in the end even necessitate one another. Now it is conceivable that all individual rights, *e.g.* of person and property, might be brought under the general conception of liberty. But we need not press this point. We may assume that there will be various rights of the individual, of the family, and so forth, which owe their validity to the functions they perform in the harmonious development of society. It is clear too that the effective exercise of the common will is also for some purposes — though for what purpose in particular may be a matter on which opinion differs — a condition of the same object. Now in general the problem of social philosophy is to define in principle, and of statesmanship to adjust in practice the bearing of these several conditions. This bearing is to be understood by considering their social value, and thus it remains to state in quite general terms the basis of the value of personal liberty on the one hand and of social control on the other. As to liberty in general, since society is made up of persons, we prove its necessity sufficiently if we show that a measure of liberty is essential to the development of personality. And since personality consists in rational determination by clear-sighted purpose as against the rule of impulse on the one side or external compulsion on the other, it follows that liberty of choice is the condition of its development. The central condition of such development is self-guidance. We should not oppose self-guidance to guidance by others for the contact with other minds is an integral part of the growth, intellectual or moral, of each mind. But we must oppose it to coercion by external sanctions, which ousts all genuinely ethical considerations and closes the door on rational choice. Liberty then is the condition of mental and moral expansion, and of all forms of associated as well as personal life that rest for their value on spontaneous feeling and the sincere response of the intellect and of the will. It is therefore the foundation not only of all that part of life which rests on personal affection, but also of science and philosophy, of religion, art, and morals.

To recognize liberty on this side is the duty of the state, but to recognize liberty is by no means to abolish restraint. On the contrary, it is only by an organized system of restraints that such liberty is made available for all members of society, for the unpopular opinions as well as the popular ones, for those whose views of life are eccentric as well as for the normal and the commonplace. Even in regard to matters of conscience it is only opinion and persuasion that can be absolutely free, and even here it must be admitted that there are forms of persuasion that are in fact coercive, and it is fair for the state to consider how far the liberty of the younger or weaker must be protected against forms of temptation which overcome the will. Apart from this when opinion leads, however conscientiously, to action, such action may coerce others, and this would bring the state into play in the name of liberty itself. It may, more generally, infringe any right and it is the business of social control to adjust one right to another.

This adjustment is simply one part, though one of the most important parts, of the general function of social control. This function may now be defined in general terms as that of securing the best conditions for the common life (*a*) so far as these are best obtained by the use of public resources and governmental machinery, (*b*) so far as such conditions are only obtainable by the use of compulsion; that is to say, where action is frustrated if it is not universal, and again where in the absence of regulation one man can directly or indirectly constrain another, infringe his rights, obstruct his rational choice, or take advantage of his weakness or ignorance. The first object includes the organization of public services by the state [1] and the provision for all its members of the external conditions of a healthy and efficient civic life. To build on this foundation is the work of the individual, and the scope of personality is increased in proportion as the conditions of its effective development are made universal. The extension of the functions of the state in this direction, accordingly, is due not to a diminished sense of personal responsibility but to a heightened sense of collective responsibility. The second case includes the laying down of certain rules, as in the adoption of general holidays, where in the absence of legal control a general desire might be thwarted by individual and perhaps quite selfish objections. It covers, again, the regulation of contract where experience has shown that the weaker party to a bargain may be forced to consent to that which, if he stood on equal terms, he would never accept. In both cases as has been shown but particularly in the latter the purpose of control is rather to define

---

[1] This, as remarked above (p. 187), does not necessarily involve compulsion, and so far does not affect the question of the limits of liberty. It does, however, intimately concern the cognate question of the limits of personal and collective responsibility.

and enlarge the sphere of liberty than to restrict it. There remains the question of those who are incapable of rational choice, — the feeble-minded or the habitual drunkard, — for whom the value of liberty does not exist. To them society owes the duties of a guardian, and in their case the policy of constraining a man for his own good is no self-contradiction, for the " good " of which they are capable is not that of personal development through the spontaneous action of thought and feeling and will, but the negative one of immunity from the dangers into which their helplessness might lead them. This is the exception proving the rule that a normal human being is not to be coerced for his own good, because as a rational being his good depends on self-determination, and is impaired or destroyed by coercion.

Thus liberty and control are not as such opposed There are borderland cases where honest thinkers must allow conflict to be possible, *e.g.* the conscientious refusal of a Friend to render military service judged to be necessary for the safety of the community. But the value of liberty is to build up the life of the mind, while the value of state control lies in securing the external conditions, including the mutual restraint, whereby the life of the mind is rendered secure. In the former sphere compulsion only defeats itself. In the latter liberty defeats itself. Hence in the main the extension of control does not impair liberty, but on the contrary is itself the means of extending liberty and may and should be conceived with that very object in view. Thus it is that upon the whole we see a tendency to the **removal of restraints in the sphere in which whatever** there is of value to mankind depends on spontaneity of impulse, free interchange of ideas, and voluntary cooperation going along with the tendency to draw tighter the bonds which restrain men from acting directly or indirectly to the injury of their fellows and to enlarge the borders of the action of the state in response to a developing sense of collective responsibility. We are dealing with two conditions of harmonious development apparently opposed and requiring themselves to be rendered harmonious by careful appreciation of their respective functions, and the general direction in which harmony is to be sought may be expressed by saying that the further development of the state lies in such an extension of public control as makes for the fuller liberty of the life of the mind.

The problem of liberty is not the only one raised by the movement of opinion which has been traced. There are far-reaching questions of economics involved, to discuss which would take us to the foundation of the right of property. Having, for reasons of time, to confine myself to one aspect of the question, I choose that of the relation of liberty to collective control because it lies at the root of the harmonic conception of society. If we are right in thinking that social evolution has brought us to a point at which the future movement of society may be subjected to rational control, it becomes at once vital to determine how far that control is to be reconciled with the old ideal of freedom.

If the above argument is just, we may conclude that the development of the common life, the collective effort, which has already been in progress in my country for a generation or more, is not adverse to the freedom, the responsibility, or the dignity of the individual. On the contrary it has in the past assisted and may in the future be expected to further the development of these essential features of a good social order. A more real freedom, a more general and more complete personal independence, a more stable because a more free family life are among the prime objects of the extension of social control. It is here that we realise the concrete meaning of the idea of harmony as the touchstone of social development. All one-sided progress cramps as much in one direction as it liberates in another. True development is not in metaphor but in essentials comparable to organic growth — the opening out of each element furthering instead of retarding that of others. Such a development, lastly, it has been my endeavor to show is not in conflict with immovable laws of evolution but is continuous with the line of advance which educed the higher from the lower animal forms, which evolved the human out of the animal species and civilized from barbaric society. The essential condition of this change was not the struggle for existence but the rise and growth of a principle of organic harmony or coöperation which from the first rise of parental care begins to mitigate and finally to restrict the field of struggle. Merely to point to the existence of this tendency was not, we admitted, sufficient to justify it, but we urged that its existence and success suffice to prove the feasibility of the conscious effort to carry through the harmonic principle in social life, and that this is in fact the guiding principle of a rational social philosophy. To apply such a principle, we admitted, is a matter of infinite practical difficulty, but it nowhere founders on any theoretic objections, for no essential element of social value has to be purchased at the expense of the fundamental and irrevocable loss of any other element of essential value. Its emergence constitutes a turning-point to which all previous progress leads up, and from which further progress will proceed with a new directness of aim and steadiness of tread. The keenest critics of the feasibility of social progress we saw rest their case on the tendency of the higher social ethics to preserve inferior types and so lead to racial deterioration. But on this point we saw that if it is true, which is not yet proved, that selection remains essential to social progress, the solution of the difficulty is to be found in the replacement of natural by social selection. At many points in the argument limitations of time have forced me to confine myself to mere illustrations of method in place of the full and lengthy statement of evidence which is requisite for proof. Those methods I would hope that some of you would follow out for yourselves, so as to verify or correct the conclusion to which I have sought to lead you. That conclusion I may be allowed to state provisionally and it is simply this: that the conception of social progress as a deliberate movement towards the reorganization of society in accordance with ethical ideas is not vitiated by any contradiction. It is free from any internal disharmony. Its possibility rests on the facts of evolution, of the higher tendencies of which it is indeed the outcome. It embodies a rational philosophy, it gives scope and meaning to the best impulses of human nature, and a new hope to the suffering among mankind.

INDEX

Action, collective, Extension of, 166
Age of Reason, The, 13
Alternatives, Choice of, 23
Arbitration, Compulsory, 170; conciliation boards of, 170
Army of men and women at work, 2-3; criticized as guerilla bands, 3-4
Ashanti, Power of the chief in, 135
Assumptions, Certain initial, 83-84
Athens, Slave-holding democracy of, 141, 142; despotism in, 142
Authority, Transmutation of force into, 137-39; the duties of, 138-39; development of citizenship at expense of, 142; power of, 147; the system of, 148

Babylon, Sanctity of the ruler in, 135; duty of the superior in, 138
Barrington, Miss Amy, and Prof. Pearson, Dogmatic conclusions of, 60-61
Bateson, The newer discoveries of, 68; on genetic knowledge, 78-79
Benthamites, Utilitarian creed of the, 167
Bias of social memory, The, 2
Biological alternative, Sufficient reason for declining the, 24
Biological conditions of human society, 13-16; not a barrier to progress, 80
Biological criticism of society, The, 22
Biological elements in a crowd, 31
Biological evolution and social progress, causes of contrast between, 28-33
Biological investigation, Darwin's impulse to, 17

Biological principles, The uncritical application of, to social progress results in contradiction, 28
Biologist, The, and the problem of social betterment, 20-25; his theory a barren tautology, 24; and the standard of value, 24-25; and sociological conditions, 67
Birth-rate, General fall in the, 15; and economic conditions, 67-68
Blending, Peculiarities of quality traceable to laws of, 69-70
Blood, The tie of, 129
Board of Trade, Demand for intervention of, in industrial disputes, 170
Bonds for human society, 128
British Empire, The, an oligarchy, 144; and its dependencies, 145
Buckle and the records of humanity, 17

Cæsar, Julius, an exceptional ruler, 136
Capacity, Mental or spiritual, 91
Caste and class distinctions broken down by civilization, 27
Caste system, The, a product of social evolution, 8
Change, Every, provokes reactions, 6
Chief, Development of the powers of the, 134-35
Child, unborn, Effect of influences on mother upon the, 63-64
Childhood, a period of helplessness, 176
Child-labor, Restriction of, 168-69
Children, The home environment of, 57-60; intelligence of, 58-59
Children of infected stocks, Prevention of, 42, 43

INDEX

Chinese theory of government, The, 137, 138

Choice, Human, an actual force in the evolution of society, 82

Citizen, Duty of the, to the state, 184

Citizenship, The principle of, 139–48; the citizens are the state, 139–40; earliest form of state, 141; the city state incapable of expansion, 142–43; conquest incompatible with, 143–44; the problem of nationality, 146–47; union rendered possible by, 147–48; the system of, 148; opposed to force, 149

City state, The, of ancient Greece, 141–43

Civilization, The history of, 13; measuring the movement of, 126; for the first time has the upper hand in our own day, 163; a new type of, 164

Civil Service, Result of reform of the, 183

Clan and commune, The simple life of, cancelled by force and authority, 149

Class distinctions defended on eugenic grounds, 47

Classification, of a social morphology, 118–20; true affinities in a, 124

Collective activity, Great extension of, 184

Common life, The conception of a, extended to the community, 152–53; securing the best conditions for the, the function of social control, 200–2; development of the, not adverse to the freedom of the individual, 203–4

Compulsion of the state on the individual, 187–88; kind of, necessary, 188–89, 201

Comte and the records of humanity, 17

Contract, Evils from the régime of free, 182; regulation of, 201–2

Control over nature the root of social inequality, 163

Coöperation, the ideal of harmonious development, 185; how far social, can be furthered by the state, 189; ineffective, 194; rise and growth of principle of, 204

Coöperators, 4

Crime, Diminution of, 50

Criminology, The imperfectly solved problems of, 151

Criticism, Common characteristics of literary, 1

Crowd, The social phenomenon of a, 30–32; interaction of personal forces in a, 31; at a London crossing, 32

Custom, Sacredness of, in the primitive community, 137

Custom and authority, Order produced by, 32–33

Customs maintained by the social tradition control the individual, 94; difference between laws and, 140–41

Dahomey, Power of the chief in, 135

Darwin, Relation of, to evolution, 17–18; and Newton, 18; main effect of work of, 18–19; his conception of the struggle for existence, 107; and social evolution, 112–13

DeVries, The newer discoveries of, 68

Death-rate, Decline of the, 50

Decay of nations, The, lacks historical proof, 53

Dependencies, The government of, 144–45

Despotic principle, The, in a free community, 142

Destitution, The test of, eliminated, 172, 174

Deterioration, physical, Committee on, 49–50; process of, not begun, 51

Development, Meaning of, 84–85; involves quantitative growth and increase, 85; how harmonious, applies, 91; lines of a significant, 147

Development, harmonious, Ideal of, is coöperation, 185; many conditions of social welfare under, 198–99; two conditions of, 203; comparable to organic growth, 204

INDEX

Disestablishment, Little headway for, in England, 181

Disestablishment of the English Church in Wales, Agitation for the, 181

East, Rise of a new spirit in the, 144

Education, Effect of, 57

Education, public, The State and, 180-82

Egypt, Ancient, Sanctity of the ruler in, 135; credit for beneficence claimed by rulers in, 139

Elderton, Ethel M., "The Relative Strength of Nurture and Nature," 55 n.; on measuring the effect of environment, 57-60.

Elimination of the unsuccessful, 53-55

Empire, One man cannot govern a great, 136

Endogamy, The principle of, 132

Environment, Improvement of, has no effect on the stock, 49, 55; assumption that, meant race progress, 55; effect of, 56-60; the social, must be established upon ethical lines, 74

Equality, Question of meaning of, 151-52

Ethical ideas and evolutionary processes, 9-10; advance of, 39

Ethical principles cannot be mutilated, 27; advance of, 39

Ethics, The highest, 23

Eugenics, The new doctrine of, 28; value and limitations of, 40-79; needs for success in, 42-43; the case of, at its strongest, 43-44; application of, to the feeble-minded, 45-46; on physiological or medical lines, 46; class distinctions a basis for, 46-48; political eugenists, 48; possible true problem of, 69-70; the general problem of, 71

Eugenists, The insistent school of, 4

Evils, Persistent efforts to discover and eradicate causes of, 2-4

Evolution defined as any sort of growth, 8; no proof of goodness, 8; and progress, not the same thing, 11; the conception of, 16; not confined to biology, 17; progress to be compared with the actual course of, 80; Darwin and, 112-14; a process from the simple to the complex, 114

Evolution and progress, 149-65; the study of, tells us what may be, 158; the inductive theory of, lies at the back of any sound social philosophy, 165

Exogamy, The principle of, 131-32

Family, The mean size of the, 64-65; causes of the limitation of the, 66; has no connection with social legislation, 67; best form of organization of, 89; in lower forms of society, 129-31; the paternal, affords a more solid basis for social order, 133

Family unity, The ideal of, 89

Father, The position of the, dominates the family, 129-30

Father-right, and mother-right, Blending of, 133-34

Feeble-minded, Application of eugenics to the, 45-46, 76; society owes the duties of a guardian to the, 202

Fertility, of the poorer classes, 46, 48; table of comparative, 64; and individual development vary inversely, 65; diminished, no argument against ameliorative legislation, 68

Fit, Who are the, 22; a hopeless missfit term, 24, 52-53; sterility of the, 48; propagation of the, should be encouraged, 49; birth-rate of the, diminishing, 72; can find their place, 76.

"Fit" nation, The eugenic would evolve a, 77

Fluctuations not permanently transmitted, 68

Force, not a basis of social life, 136; transmuted into authority, 137, 147

Freedom, from alien government, 190-91

INDEX

Functions, Moral and spiritual, of the state, 188; the legitimate, 188–89; sphere of, how determined, 189; corollary to ethical basis of, 191
Generic forms and specific types, 113
Genetics, Sociological application of the science of, 77; Professor Bateson on, 78–79
Germ-plasm, Possible effects of influences on the, 62–64
Good for man, The, how found, 83–84
Government, The growth of, and its relation to liberty, 125; of Bentham's day, a close and corrupt corporation, 183
Greco-Roman culture maintained a losing fight against barbarization, 163
Greek freedom, Real loss in the destruction of, 159, 160
Group-morality, 26–28; the ideal of, self-contradictory, 27; obligations of, less than those of common morality, 27
Growth of the state, The, 126–48
Guerilla bands of inefficient workers, 3–4

Happiness, Some form of, good, 83; the idea of, 92
Harmonic principle, The, in social life, 204; its emergence a turning-point, 205
Harmony, between the claims of different persons, 86–87; in the manifold developments of life, 92–93; conditions of, 93; essential conditions of, realized, 153; in the development of personal life, 185; the touchstone of social development, 204
Harvard graduates, Low fertility of, 65
Health, Improvement of general, 50
Hellenic civilization, a tiny islet in a world of far lower culture, 163
Heredity remains though traditions change, 37–38
Hierarchies, Variety of, 138
Highland clan, Powers of the chief in the, 134

Historic progress, Interpretation of, 156
Hours of labor limited by law, 169
Housing and sanitary reform, Apostles of, 4
Human beings, Malthus' law of increase of, 14
Human nature, The state inadequate to the subtlety of, 187
Humanitarian feeling, A deepening of, 183–84
Humanity, Continuous deterioration of, may be proved from literature, 1; ups and downs of, 13; the supreme society, 88; development of, the directing principle of human endeavor, 155
Hunter, The primitive, and the modern laborer, 160
Hypothesis, A good evolutionary, 113; legitimate vs. illegitimate use of, 113

Ideals, Conflict of, 185
Ideas, Propagation of, in three ways, 36; precede the means of expression, 93
Idler, Provision for the determined, 179–80
Imitation not a simple term, 35; two types of, 36–37
Incidence of taxation, 67
Individual, Not the inherent qualities but the actual life of the, to be regarded, 62; the average, 75; manifold relations of each, 88; controlled by the customs of social tradition, 94; a member and servant of the society of mankind, 155; relation of the, to the state, an unsolved problem, 166–70; sphere of collective responsibility for welfare of, extended, 180; and the state, 185–205; ultimate liberty of an, in the state, 187; rights of the, 189, 196–98; interest of the, opposed to that of all, 194–95; basis of liberty of the, 196–98
Individual, Relation between the, and society, 56

INDEX

Individual development and fertility vary inversely, 65
Individual enterprise, Sphere of, 196
Individuals, Qualities of, determined the nature of their interactions, 40, 41; society composed of, 29, 40; variations of, 69; society exists in, 85; social relations of, 85
Industrial contracts, Growth of public control over, 168–70
Industrial development, Steps of, readily traced, 154
Industrial regulation, Extension of public responsibility in, 168–70
Industrial training, A system of, for the unemployed, 180
Infantile death-rate, Decline of the, 49
Infertility of the best stocks, 64
Inheritance, Competent knowledge of laws of, 42
"Inheritance of Vision, The," by Miss Barrington and Prof. Pearson, 60–62
Insanity, Increase of, 51
Institutions, Analogical resemblances between, 122–23; the principle or spirit of, to be examined, 124; conditions traced in the history of, 156; definite, the life of the state, 186–87
Insurance against unemployment. Scheme of, 178
Intellectuals, English, Low fertility of, 65
Intelligence of children measured, 58–59
Interaction of human beings the fundamental fact of social life, 30, 31, 33, 40
Interest, Individual, opposed to collective, 194–95
Interests, Mutuality of, 127–28
Internationalism, Development of the civic principle bound up with, 145
Interplay of human motives, 33
Ireland, Increase of lunacy in, 51 n.
Irish Church, Disestablishment of the, 181
Iroquois, The totemic and tribal bonds of the, 133

Japan, Rise of, 144
Jones, Henry, on relation between the individual and society, 56
Judgment, No progress without the approval of rational, 11
Jus connubii, 132
Justice, Social and economic, as eugenic agencies, 53; evolution of the idea of, 150–51; a means of maintaining right and redressing wrong, 151; of impartial, 152

King, The actual power of a, limited, 136; the fountain of justice, 137
Kinship, in lower forms of society, 129; relation of mother and children, 129; the patriarchate, 129–30; mother-right, 130–31; exogamy, 131–32; endogamy, 132; the paternal family the stronger basis of, 133; the ties of, 147, 148; the system of, 148
Knowledge, The development of, 154
Knowledge and industry, Rapid and certain advance in, 39

Labor, State control over, 167–70
Labor colony for idlers, 179
Labor exchanges, The, and the unemployed, 179–80
Laissez-faire principle, Predominance of the, 168
Land questions, Enthusiasts find, at the root of all good and evil, 3–4
Language a social product, 93
Law, A, in science, and in social evolution, 103–6; the true, of evolution, 106
Law as a rule imposed by a superior, 191; as the expression of a general resolve, 191–92
Laws, State, 186; have force behind them, 187
Liberals and Radicals, The older school of English, advocated restricting the sphere of the state, 167
Liberty, The ultimate, of individuals in a voluntary association and in a state, 187; no social, without social restraint, 189; as a social

conception, 189–90; a problem of organizing restraints, 190; as the right of self-expression, a right masses may claim, 192; of the individual, 196–98; as a restraint upon society, 196; necessity of, 199; final definition of, 200; recognition of, does not abolish restraints, 200; and control not opposed, 202–3

Liberty, personal, Basis of the value of, 199–200

Liberty, Political and civil, as eugenic agencies, 53; conception of, 166; of the individual, 166–67; question of kind of, 182

Life, human, Possibility of a harmonious development of, no dream, 165

Life, Some kind of, good for man, 83; the fuller, the more desirable, 83, 91

Life, The higher, a result of mutual aid, 23

London crossing, Crowd handled at a, 32

Lower Empire, Declining ages of the, 159

Lyer, Dr. Müller, "Phasen der Kultur," 126

Majorities, The rights of, 192; may be denied, 192–94; self-expression for, through machinery of law, 193; right of, defeated, 194

Malthus' law of population, 13–14

Malthusians, The, 14–15

Man reacts to new circumstances, 15; moved by the knowledge of ends, 16; the dominant animal, 25; questions about, 115–16; sciences which deal with, 116

Manchester School, National liberty the center of all things to the, 167

Marriage, Types of, 120–23; in ancient Rome, 132; extension of rights of, 132

Mating, Selective, the possible true problem of eugenics, 69–70

Maudlin sentiment, 21

Medieval city, Real loss in the decay of the, 159

Men of the reindeer period, Disappearance of the, 162

Merovingian period, Barbaric anarchy of the, 159

Metal, sheet of, with a dint in, Spencer's illustration of the, 5–6

Miner's Act, The English, 169

Misery an evil, 83

Mother, Effect of influences on the, upon the unborn child, 63–64

Mother and children, The relation of, 129–31

Mother-right, Descent by, 130–31; the natural family never complete under, 133

Mothers, The universal property of, 129

Mudge, G. P., reviewing Bateson in the *Eugenic Review*, 77

Mutations, of permanent significance, 68; definite, the basis of racial progress, 70–71

Mutual aid, the persistent enemy of progress, 22–23; voluntary organization of, 191

Napoleon an exceptional ruler, 136

Nationality, A common, 140; the problem of, in the state, 146–47; the sentiment of, 146

Natural rights, A social order founded on, 13

Natural selection, Assumption that the universe progresses by, 9; Darwin's principle of, 18–19; the foundation of all progress, 22; restricted by mutual aid, 23; replaced by rational, 28, 41; defended by the political eugenists, 48–49; suspension of, 49; does suspension of, lower the racial standard, 51–55; a permanent necessity of racial progress, 70; Darwin's theory of, 113–14; probable triumphs of, 162; replaced by social selection, 205

Nature and nurture, 55–56, 57; no adequate means of measurement of, 61–62

INDEX

Neolithic and Paleolithic epochs, 162–63

Nicholas I and Russia governed by clerks, 136

Old age not the only period of helplessness, 176

Old Age Pensions Act of 1908, 173–74; principle of the, 175; arguments against and for, 175–76

Opinion, The actual movement of, 184; in the light of social theory, 185

Optimism, Speculative, of the eighteenth century, 13

Orange Colony, Autonomy extended to the, 144

Orbit, Determining an, 105

Order, Extension and solidity of, 152; the most stable, based on freedom, 152–53; antithesis between, and liberty, 183

Organism, An, is a whole consisting of interdependent parts, 87

Organization, Improved, does not imply improved individuals, 30 n.

Oriental civilizations subject to deluges of barbarism, 163

Orientals, Principles of liberty cannot be denied to the, 145

Pan-Hellenic sentiment and the spirit of autonomy, 164

Parentage, The claim to, 42; a case for forbidding, 45

Parental love, The operation of, 23

Parental responsibility, Increased sense of, 66–67; undermined, 89; limits of sphere of, 89; failure of, in education, 90; and the state, 90

Past, The, appears in a halo of romance, 1–2

Patriarchate, The, 130

Pauper, The problem of the, 171–72

Pauperism, Decline of, 50; a hereditary taint, 74–75

Pearson, Professor, "The Problem of Practical Eugenics," 64; see also Barrington, Miss Amy and

Pensions, Old Age, 173–76; for other periods of helplessness proposed, 176–78

Personal experience, how made up, 94

Personal liberty, Restrictions of, 181; basis of the value of, 199–200

Personality defined, 199–200

Pessimism, Note of, in literature of the day, 1–3

Philosophy of history, 17

Physical conditions influencing action of a crowd, 31

Poor Law Commission of 1834, Views of the, 170–71

Poor Law Commission, Report of, in 1909, 172; views of the minority, 172

Poor Law Reports criticized by the eugenics, 72–73

Position in society, Forces which determine a man's, 47–48

Poverty, provision for, Change in public opinion on, 170–72

Prestige, A scientific, 18

Prevention and cure, Principles of, 151

Primitive man the victim of natural selection, 162

Process of things has nothing to do with value, 9

Progress, Meaning of, 1–16; preliminary definition of, 7–9; difference between evolution and, 7–8, 11–12; a possibility of evolution, 8; connotes value, 9; the realization of an ethical order, 12; objection to, founded on history, 12–13; the biological argument, 13; Malthus' natural law, 13–15; new difficulties, 16; and the struggle for existence, 17–39; standard of value of, 24; not racial but social, 39; depends on survival of the best, 54–55; human, social not racial, 65, 80; a definition of, required, 80; the movement by which harmony is realized, 93; real and fundamental, 152; the work of, unfinished, 153; the realization of the conditions of full social coöperation, 156; a genuine

possibility, 159; an optimistic belief in, may be nursed, 159; theory of continuous automatic inevitable, impossible, 160; the positive view of, 161; uneven nature of, intelligible, 162
Progress of organic forms by a continuous struggle for existence, 18–19
Property, Respect for, 123
Prophecies the causes of their own fulfilment, 81
Psychology, Comparative, 116–17; the of, 117
Psychology of a crowd, 30–31, 35; all higher, social, 93
Public assistance as a preventive, 172–73
Public works should be laid out for the unemployed, 178

Qualities, Social order the outcome of individual, 41; that should be extinguished, 43; that bring men to the top, 47–48
Quality, Is a distinct, impressed on the individual, perpetuated in the stock? 62–64

Race, The, has been relatively stagnant, 39; doomed, 49; effect on, of breeding inferior stocks, 68
Race, The, of higher powers, enslaves the weaker, 163
Race and environment, 55, 64
Race deterioration, Absence of inductive evidence of, 51
Race suicide, Alarmist talk of, 16
Racial and social progress, Distinction between, 55–57
Racial level, The, 41
Racial progress dependent on definite mutations, 68–69
Racial standard, Variations of the, 52–53
Rates, Burden of the, 67–68
Rational selection, to replace natural selection, 28, 41, 75; a legitimate object, 41
Redress for the individual becomes the concern of government, 151

Reformers, Efforts of, not wasted, 3; the sectional spirit among, 3–4; work of, accomplished at vast expense and waste, 4
Religion, Bond of a common, 128
Representation, The principle of, in the modern state, 143
Reproduction, Qualitative vs. quantitative, 66
Resemblances, Analogical, 122–23
Responsibility, Deepening sense of collective, 183–84, 201, 203
Retaliation, The idea of, limited to compensation or restitution, 151
Right, Meaning of a, 196–98; correlative of a duty, 196; legal, moral, or ethical, 197; any genuine, a condition of social welfare, 198
Rights enforced by society, Question of what, 151; the common good the foundation of all personal, 198; natural, 197–98; all individual, included in liberty, 199
Roman, The, civilized enough to recognize Hellenic superiority, 163
Roman decadence, Half-told tale of, 53–54
Roman population, Lamentations over decay of, unfounded, 53
Roman state, Deep-seated injury in the breakup of the, 159; could not reconcile liberty with empire, 164
Ruler, Divine right of the, 137
Russia governed by ten thousand clerks, 136

Savage and civilized man, Life of, compared, 12–13
Science is social knowledge and has permanency, 95
Secondary education provided, 181
Sectional spirit, The driving force of all with the, 4
Selection necessary to racial progress, 41–42
Self-guidance, 199–200
Sensitiveness to social ailments widely diffused, 2–3
Shops, Early closing of, 194
Sickness and invalidity, Scheme of insurance for, before Parliament, 177

INDEX 215

Slave or serf, The, compares unfavorably with the free savage, 160

Social betterment, The true problem of, to the biologist, 20–25

Social bond, Nature of the, 126; mutual interest, 127–28; principles of social union, 128

Social changes, Interrelation of, 3–4; character and rapid development of, 38; determined by modifications of traditions, 39

Social conscience a factor in progress, 48

Social control, Basis of the value of, 199; business of, to adjust one right to another, 200; the function of, defined, 200–2; of those incapable of rational choice, 202; liberty and, not opposed, 202–3; prime objects of extension of, 204

Social coöperation, Ordered, 76, 148; changes for advancement of, 152

Social development distinct from the organic changes known to biology, 29; biological factors have little share in, 38; is good, 83; is individual development, 85; a movement towards a fuller life, 85; involves the harmonious development of the constituent members of society, 87, 91–92; a very wide genus, 92; not in conflict with the laws of evolution, 204

Social effort, Object of, the realization of ethical ends, 11

Social evolution, The subject-matter of, 7; defined, 8; a caste system a product of, 8; a process in, not a phase of, social progress, 8–10; treated by sociological methods, 17; the fundamental fact of, 33, 40; tendency of the changes in, 102; ambiguity of the term law of, 103; two objects for the student of, 107; the broad trend of, 107; the permanent conditions of the actual movement of society, 108; a formula of synthesis, 108–9; relation of the history of science to, 109–10; to find unity in, no simple matter, 110; of a country, a part of the evolution of civilization, 110; we must admit divergent lines of, 111; a morphology the foundation of, 111–12; Darwin and, 112–13; eminently tortuous, 149; irregular and incomplete, 151–52; ultimate reality of, 154; ends in a demand for a social philosophy, 164; history of, ends in a problem, 166; point reached by, 203

Social fact, The, distinct from the biological and the psychological, 33

Social group, Survival value of the, 25–26; each, has its claim to share in social development, 88

Social harmony and the social mind, 80–101

Social history controlled by intelligence, 165

Social improvement not the same as racial improvement, 40

Social institutions, Effect of, not to be understood in biological terms, 56

Social legislation, Eugenic writers on, 71–72; should aim at social coöperation, 76

Social life, The fundamental fact of, 33, 40; the whole fabric of society persists in, 37; good, 83; of secondary moment, 84

Social life of mankind, Harmonious development of the, 156; problems of, solved by rational methods of control, 166; essentially a coöperation, 185; mutual aid and mutual harmony essential to, 186; functions of the state within the, 186

Social mind, Definition of the term, 97; function of the, 98; a consciousness of unity, 99; development of the, a measure of progress, 100–1; germinal condition and relative maturity of the, 153–54; development of the, increases harmony, 154; genuine growth of, 155; arriving at the point of self-determination, 158; evolution of a higher, 161; progressively less liable to destruction, 162; harmonious development by the ma-

216 INDEX

turing of the, 164; sphere of the control of, greater, 165

Social morphology, 102-25; a "law" in science, 103; a descriptive synthesis, 103-6; the law of evolution, 106; Spencer on evolution, 107; Darwin on growth of species, 107; two objects for the student of evolution, 107-8; the formula of synthesis, 109-10; divergent lines of evolution, 111; Darwin and Natural Selection, 112-14; questions about Man, 115-16; Comparative Psychology and Sociology, 116-18; classification, 118-20; types of marriage, 120-23; the true affinities in classification, 124; the growth of government and its relation to liberty, 125

Social organisms, The unity of, 4-5

Social organization must be taken into account, 29-30; must be just and equitable, 55; total character of the, 62

Social phenomenon, The, an interaction of individuals, 30; of a crowd, 30-32

Social philosophy, An articulate, needed, 6; the subject-matter of, 7; a well-grounded, needed, 43, 82; what a complete exposition of, would involve, 83; demand for a, 164; an effort to form a purpose to guide the future, 165; the inductive theory of evolution at the back of any sound, 165; and moral problems, 166-84; and the relation of the individual to the state, 166; industrial regulation, 168-71; Old Age Pensions, 173-77; public education, 180-81; political changes, 182-83; question propounded to, 184; the general problem of, 199

Social progress, Clearer ideas of, needed, 4; defined, 8; not a process in evolution, 8-10; to be investigated by biological methods, 19-21; essentially an improvement of the stock, 29; implies racial development, 38; interfered with, by elimination of best types, 53-55; a certain measure of, established, 157; aim of comparative sociology to measure, 164; consists in harmonious development, 185; conception of, not vitiated by any contradiction, 205; embodies a rational philosophy, 205

Social relations, Proper adjustment of, 90

Social theory, Movement of opinion in the light of, 185

Social tradition, 33, 40

Social union, Leading principles of, 128; kinship, 129-34; authority, 134-39; citizenship, 139-48

Social welfare, Conditions of, 198-99

Social will, Existence of a, 95-96

Social worth, A true conception of, 42; two lines of thought on, 43

Socialists, 4

Society, Herbert Spencer on, 5-6; evolution of, no proof of progress, 8-9; consists of individuals, 29; has rapidly developed, 39; the broad duty of, eugenically, 55; the organic conception of, 87; a very complex structure, 88-90; the ideal development of, 89; Plato on, 164; as a guardian, 202; the reorganization of, according to ethical ideas, 205

Society, modern, Forces which determine a man's position in, 47

Sociological effects, The reaction of, unescapable, 28

Sociology, Specialism a necessity and a danger in, 6; made a science by the principle of survival of the fittest, 19; not the same as either biology or psychology, 30; deals with results of interplay of motives, 33; deals with man, 116; the prime object of, 118

Sociology, comparative, The aim of, 164

Spain, Political and religious denudation of best stocks in, 54

Sparta, a close oligarchy, 141, 142

Specialism, Danger of, in sociology, 6

Spencer, Herbert, on society as a sheet of metal with a dint in, 5-6;

INDEX

general law of fertility and development, 65; his conception of evolution, 107

Stagnation and retrogression, Long periods of, in history, 159

State action, the combined will of individuals, 191

State activity urged by the democratic element in politics, 167

State control, Extension of, not indiscriminate, 181

State, Growth of the, 126–48; mutuality of interests, 127–28; principles of social union, 128; kinship, 129–34; authority, 134–39; citizenship, 139–48; the citizens are the, 139–40; resembles the commune, 140; characteristics of the, 141; the city, of ancient Greece, 141–43; problems of the modern, 143; government of dependencies, 144–45; problem of nationality, 146–47; evolution of the, illustrates the social movement, 149; various forms of, 150; a problem, 150; relation of the, to the individual, 166–70; restriction of sphere of the, 167; extension of responsibility of the, 167–70; provision for the poor, 170–73; Old Age Pensions, 173–76; and the unemployed, 177–80; and public education, 180–81; political changes in the, 182–84; responsibility of, for the individual, 184; definite institutions the life of the, 186–87; a compulsory form of association, 187; legitimate functions of the, 188–89; how far coöperation can be furthered by the, 189; principal sphere of the, 195–96; duty of the, to recognize personal liberty, 200; organization of public services by the, 201; and provision for efficient civic life, 201

State, modern, Foreign relations of the, 145; the dominant type of society, 150; how differentiated from earlier forms of society, 166

Statesmanship, The general problem of, 199

Sterility of the richer classes, 46; of the fit, 48, 64

Stock, Good, 61; the pathological, 64–65

Stocks, Infected, not wanted, 43; we must be certain of irremovable viciousness of, 45, 75

Stocks, inferior, Multiplication of, 64; possibilities of, 70

Strains, Many fundamental, intricately blended, 69

Struggle for existence, A continuous, 18–19; the biologist and the, 19–25; conception of, modified, 25; between communities, 26; elimination of best types in severe, 53–55

Subordination, The principle of, 137–38

Subvention, Public, to the needs of poverty, 178

Suffrage, Benefits of extension of the, 183

Suffrage, Roman, Extension of, 142

Superior, The, has duties as well as privileges, 138–39

Suppression, The idea of, extended to that of punishment and retaliation, 150–51

Survival value of the social group, 25–26

Synthesis, Descriptive, in evolution, 103–5; and true law, 106; the formula of, 108–10, 116

Tariff reformers, 4

Temperance specialists care for nothing else, 3

Tendency, Existence of a, does not make it desirable, 81; some, desirable, 82

Thebes a close oligarchy, 142

Thought, The, of any generation, a social product, 94–95; development of, 154–55; comparative study of ethico-religious, 155; extension of the rational control of life traced in the history of, 156

Thrift, Enthusiasts for, 3

Tiberius, Emperor, and the provincial governor, 136

Trade Unionists, 4
Tradition the main subject of sociological inquiry, 33–35, 40; analogous to heredity in the individual, 34; hands on the whole social environment, 35; growth of, modifies individuals, 37
Transvaal, Autonomy extended to the, 144
Tubercle, The, not tubercular stock, should be eliminated, 44–45,
Tuberculosis involves no mental or moral turpitude, 44

Unemployment, Treatment of, in the Poor Law Reports, 73–74; due to various causes, 171; public provision for, 177–78; scheme of insurance against, 178; the labor exchanges and, 179–80
Unfit, Elimination of the hopelessly, 78; survival of the, 162
Unfitness, how proven, 76
Universalism, A code of, a step to deterioration, 26–27
Universe, Assumptions of progress of the, 9, 20

Variation, Wide limits of, for society, 40

Wages, Rise in real, 50; government regulation of, 169–70; difference of, in good and bad years, 178
Wages boards, Action of, limited, 170
Waste of effort, How to avoid, 4–5
Wastrels, 74
Webb, Sidney, on low fertility of English intellectuals, 65
Whetham, W. C. D., quoted, 9
Wigglesworth, Dr., on increase of insanity, 51
Will, the general, Restraint of, 196–97; the effective exercise of the, a condition of harmonious development, 199
Wisdom, true, The beginning of, 84
Women, New opportunities opened to, 65–66
Women's labor, question of, 168–69
World state, How a, is to be achieved, 91; possibility of a, 148

Zulus, Principles of liberty cannot be denied to the, 145

C. A. NELSON.

COLUMBIA UNIVERSITY PRESS
Columbia University in the City of New York

The Press was incorporated June 8, 1893, to promote the publication of the results of original research. It is a private corporation, related directly to Columbia University by the provisions that its Trustees shall be officers of the University and that the President of Columbia University shall be President of the Press.

The publications of the Columbia University Press include works on Biography, History, Economics, Education, Philosophy, Linguistics, and Literature, and the following series:

Columbia University Contributions to Anthropology.
Columbia University Biological Series.
Columbia University Studies in Cancer and Allied Subjects.
Columbia University Studies in Classical Philology.
Columbia University Studies in Comparative Literature.
Columbia University Studies in English.
Columbia University Geological Series.
Columbia University Germanic Studies.
Columbia University Indo-Iranian Series.
Columbia University Contributions to Oriental History and Philology.
Columbia University Oriental Studies.
Columbia University Studies in Romance Philology and Literature.

Adams Lectures.   Carpentier Lectures.
Julius Beer Lectures.   Hewitt Lectures.
Blumenthal Lectures.   Jesup Lectures.

Catalogues will be sent free on application.

LEMCKE & BUECHNER, AGENTS
30-32 EAST 20th ST., NEW YORK

COLUMBIA UNIVERSITY PRESS
Columbia University in the City of New York

COLUMBIA UNIVERSITY LECTURES

ADAMS LECTURES

GRAPHICAL METHODS. By Carl Runge, Ph.D., Professor of Applied Mathematics in the University of Göttingen; Kaiser Wilhelm Professor of German History and Institutions for the year 1909–1910. 8vo, cloth, pp. ix + 148. Price, $1.75 *net*.

JULIUS BEER LECTURES

SOCIAL EVOLUTION AND POLITICAL THEORY. By Leonard T. Hobhouse, Professor of Sociology in the University of London. 12mo, cloth, pp. ix + 218. Price, $2.00 *net*.

BLUMENTHAL LECTURES

POLITICAL PROBLEMS OF AMERICAN DEVELOPMENT. By Albert Shaw, LL.D., Editor of the *Review of Reviews*. 12mo, cloth, pp. vii + 268. Price, $2.00 *net*.

CONSTITUTIONAL GOVERNMENT IN THE UNITED STATES. By Woodrow Wilson, LL.D., sometime President of Princeton University. 12mo, cloth, pp. vii + 236. Price, $2.00 *net*.

THE PRINCIPLES OF POLITICS FROM THE VIEWPOINT OF THE AMERICAN CITIZEN. By Jeremiah W. Jenks, LL.D., Professor of Government and Public Administration in New York University. 12mo, cloth, pp. xviii + 187. Price, $2.00 *net*.

THE COST OF OUR NATIONAL GOVERNMENT. By Henry Jones Ford, Professor of Politics in Princeton University. 12mo, cloth, pp. xv + 147. Price, $2.00 *net*.

THE BUSINESS OF CONGRESS. By Hon. Samuel W. McCall, Member of Congress for Massachusetts. 12mo, cloth, pp. vii + 215. Price, $2.00 *net*.

THOMAS JEFFERSON: HIS PERMANENT INFLUENCE ON AMERICAN INSTITUTIONS. By Hon. John Sharp Williams, United States Senator from Mississippi. 12mo, cloth, pp. ix + 330. Price, $2.00 *net*.

LEMCKE & BUECHNER, Agents
30–32 EAST 20th ST., NEW YORK

COLUMBIA UNIVERSITY PRESS
Columbia University in the City of New York

COLUMBIA UNIVERSITY LECTURES

OUR CHIEF MAGISTRATE AND HIS POWERS. By WILLIAM HOWARD TAFT, Twenty-seventh President of the United States. 12mo, cloth, pp. vii + 165. Price, $2.00 *net*.

CONSTITUTIONAL POWER AND WORLD AFFAIRS. By GEORGE SUTHERLAND, former United States Senator from Utah. 12mo, cloth, pp. vii + 202. Price, $2.00 *net*.

CARPENTIER LECTURES

WORLD ORGANIZATION AS AFFECTED BY THE NATURE OF THE MODERN STATE. By HON. DAVID JAYNE HILL, sometime American Ambassador to Germany. 12mo, cloth, pp. ix + 214. Price, $2.00 *net*.

THE GENIUS OF THE COMMON LAW. By the RT. HON. SIR FREDERICK POLLOCK, Bart., D.C.L., LL.D., Bencher of Lincoln's Inn, Barrister-at-Law. 12mo, cloth, pp. vii + 141. Price, $2.00 *net*.

THE MECHANICS OF LAW MAKING. By COURTNEY ILBERT, G.C.B., Clerk of the House of Commons. 12mo, cloth, pp. viii + 209. Price, $2.00 *net*.

HEWITT LECTURES

THE PROBLEM OF MONOPOLY. By JOHN BATES CLARK, LL.D., Professor of Political Economy, Columbia University. 12mo, cloth, pp. vi + 128. Price, $1.60 *net*.

POWER. By CHARLES EDWARD LUCKE, Ph.D., Professor of Mechanical Engineering, Columbia University. 12mo, cloth, pp. vii + 316. Illustrated. Price, $2.50 *net*.

THE DOCTRINE OF EVOLUTION. Its Basis and its Scope. By HENRY EDWARD CRAMPTON, Ph.D., Professor of Zoölogy, Columbia University. 12mo, cloth, pp. ix + 311. Price, $2.00 *net*.

MEDIEVAL STORY AND THE BEGINNINGS OF THE SOCIAL IDEALS OF ENGLISH-SPEAKING PEOPLE. By WILLIAM WITHERLE LAWRENCE, Ph.D., Associate Professor of English, Columbia University. 12mo, cloth, pp. xiv + 236. Price, $2.00 *net*.

LEMCKE & BUECHNER, AGENTS
30-32 EAST 20th ST., NEW YORK

COLUMBIA UNIVERSITY PRESS
Columbia University in the City of New York

COLUMBIA UNIVERSITY LECTURES

JESUP LECTURES

LIGHT. By RICHARD C. MACLAURIN, LL.D., Sc.D., late President of the Massachusetts Institute of Technology. 12mo, cloth, pp. ix + 251. Portrait and figures. Price, $2.00 *net*.

SCIENTIFIC FEATURES OF MODERN MEDICINE. By FREDERIC S. LEE, Ph.D., Dalton Professor of Physiology, Columbia University. 12mo, cloth, pp. vii + 183. Price, $2.00 *net*.

HEREDITY AND SEX. By THOMAS HUNT MORGAN, Ph.D., Professor of Experimental Zoölogy in Columbia University. 12mo, cloth, pp. vii + 282. Illustrated. Price, $2.50 *net*.

DYNAMIC PSYCHOLOGY. By ROBERT SESSIONS WOODWORTH, Ph.D., Professor of Psychology, Columbia University. 12mo, cloth, pp. ix + 210. Price, $2.00 *net*.

FOUR STAGES OF GREEK RELIGION. By GILBERT MURRAY, Regius Professor of Greek, in the University of Oxford. 8vo, cloth, pp. 223. Price, $2.25 *net*.

LECTURES ON SCIENCE, PHILOSOPHY AND ART. A series of twenty-one lectures descriptive in non-technical language of the achievements in Science, Philosophy and Art. Published as separate pamphlets. 8vo, paper. Price, $.35 each.

LECTURES ON LITERATURE. A series of eighteen lectures by instructors of the University on literary art and on the great literatures of the world, ancient and modern. 8vo, cloth, pp. viii + 404. Price, $2.50 *net*.

GREEK LITERATURE. A series of ten lectures delivered at Columbia University by scholars from various universities. 8vo, cloth, pp. vii + 306. Price, $2.50 *net*.

THE FEDERAL INCOME TAX. A series of ten lectures by prominent experts on the income tax. Edited by ROBERT MURRAY HAIG, Ph.D., Associate Professor, School of Business, Columbia University. With an introduction by E. R. A. SELIGMAN, Professor of Political Economy, Columbia University. 8vo, cloth, pp. vi + 271. Price, $2.75 *net*.

LEMCKE & BUECHNER, AGENTS
30–32 EAST 20th ST., NEW YORK